BOREALIS BREADS

75 Recipes for Breads, Soups, Sides, and More

T0351625

·· Jim Amaral and Cynthia Finnemore Simonds ··

DownEastBooks
CAMDEN, MAINE

Down East Books

An imprint of The Rowman & Littlefield Publishing Group, Inc.
4501 Forbes Blvd., Ste. 200
Lanham, MD 20706
www.rowman.com

Distributed by NATIONAL BOOK NETWORK

British Library Cataloguing in Publication Information available

Library of Congress Cataloging-in-Publication Data available
Names: Simonds, Cynthia Finnemore, 1966– author. | Amaral, Jim, author.
Title: Borealis Breads : 75 recipes for breads, soups, sides, and more / Cynthia Finnemore Simonds and Jim Amaral.
Description: Camden, Maine : Down East Books, [2019] | Includes index.
Identifiers: LCCN 2018046538 (print) | LCCN 2018058568 (ebook) | ISBN 9781608936281 (Electronic) | ISBN 9781608936274 (cloth : alk. paper) | ISBN 9781608936281 (e-book)
Subjects: LCSH: Bread. | Cooking (Sourdough) | Baking. | Borealis Breads (Bakery) | Bakeries—Maine.
Classification: LCC TX769 (ebook) | LCC TX769 .S46 2019 (print) | DDC 641.81/5—dc23
LC record available at https://lccn.loc.gov/2018046538

♾️™ The paper used in this publication meets the minimum requirements of American National Standard for Information Sciences—Permanence of Paper for Printed Library Materials, ANSI/NISO Z39.48-1992.

Printed in the United States of America

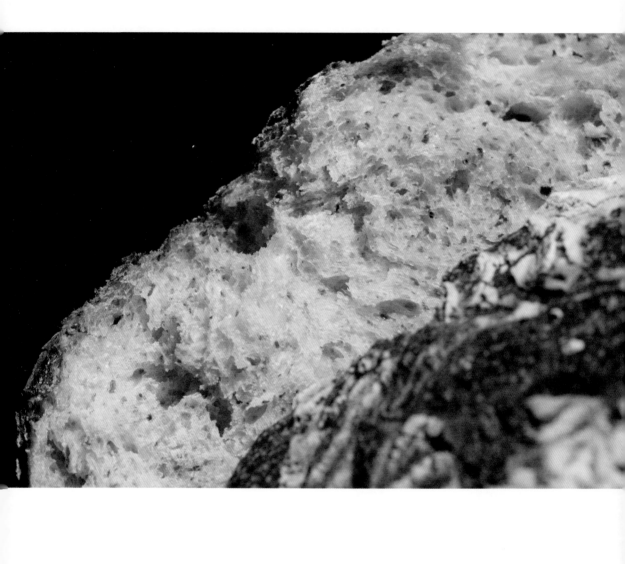

CONTENTS....

FOREWORD····

BREAD BAKING IS A TRANSFORMATIVE PROCESS. The simplest of elements—flour, water, salt, and starter—progress from ingredients to dough to bread in a way that still amazes me even after forty years of baking. The transformation extends to the baker as well. Mixing, kneading, and shaping have a meditative quality that de-stresses and energizes. Creating healthy, nutritious, delicious breads for oneself and others lends a sense of purpose and goodwill. Over the years I have had a number of folks say how much they enjoy our breads; no longer baking for themselves and their families, but choosing to purchase our bread instead. I cringe every time I hear this and want to yell, "Noooooooo, don't stop baking!"

Cynthia, a longtime dear friend, talented chef, fellow baker, and I have written this book for all those home bakers who love Borealis Breads but perhaps feel they could never bake a loaf like ours at home. It's chock-full of bread formulas that I have developed over the years, along with things to put on, in, or under your freshly home-baked loaves. Some of these breads we have been making ever since opening our doors in 1993; others are offered seasonally. Some were sold for a while but have never returned to our bread lineup, and still others, until now, have never been seen beyond my home kitchen—also known as my bread lab.

In recognition of the more than two decades of hard work that all of us have done at the bakery to use and promote locally grown grains, you will find that most of these breads contain some Maine-grown flour. A few are even made with 100 percent locally grown and sourced ingredients.

Bread in its most elemental form is a fermentative wonder that beguiles all the senses. I am not talking about those gussied-up loaves whose flavor is finessed with herbs or fruits or cheese, or whose texture is massaged with olive oil or butter, or a loaf cosseted in a pan. I'll take mine hand shaped and unconstrained by glass, ceramic, or tin. The bread of my desire is a simple concoction of four ingredients—grain, water, yeast, and salt—whose artful combination produces a hearty, hunger-slaying loaf. The grains usually, but not always, include a preponderance of wheat, which provides gluten, the bones of the bread. The water should preferably come from a well or spring. The yeast can come in many forms: sourdough starter, poolish, biga, compressed yeast, or dry yeast. Any natural salt will do.

Shall we bake and break some Maine bread together?

—*Jim Amaral*

INTRODUCTION

The Story of Borealis Breads and the Renaissance of Maine Grain

A BAKER IS BORN

IN THE SPRING OF 1993 MY WIFE, Dolores Carbonneau, and I started Borealis Breads in a small basement space under what was then the Pine Cone Café in Waldoboro village on the coast of Maine. At the time there were a few other bakers in the state practicing what has since become known as "artisan baking," including Don Stagg at Saco Bay Sourdough in downtown Saco, Mark Mickalide of Black Crow Bakery in Litchfield, and Art's Sourdough Bread Company in Sidney. Greg Larsen of Tuva Bakery in Lincolnville was upholding the hippie baking tradition with a wholesome selection of whole grain pan breads. Of the original group, only Mark carries on to produce excellent breads at his bakery. Today we have a new generation. In Lincoln County alone, I can count at least six bakers producing superb artisan breads. What a fantastic legacy!

It was only a couple of years after starting our bakery that I set out to source locally grown wheat for use in our breads. Back then I was immersed in starting the business, developing bread formulas, wooing new customers, and, of course, nurturing the sourdough starters that to this day provide the flavor foundation for our breads. I had little cognizance of what other food fermentations were beginning to slowly bubble up, or that my quest for locally produced flour would be the dawn of what has become today's vibrant local grain renaissance.

My path to becoming a bread baker started in 1971, in Concord, Massachusetts. I was a sophomore in high school and a voracious reader and book buyer. On Main Street in Concord center back then, you could find an excellent bookshop and, a few doors down, the Sally Ann Food Shop, a small retail bakery. In fact, both stores are still in operation today. That summer the bakery was looking for a pot washer, and I was looking for a way to fund my book-buying habit. During my interview I learned that the bakery employees were paid in cash every Saturday morning. Needless to say, I immediately took the job when it was offered.

I was hired to do whatever needed to be done. Washing sheet pans led to cleaning the floor with bench scrapers. Once I mastered those tasks, I moved up to sweeping and mopping. Very quickly I graduated to lugging 100-pound bags of flour up a narrow staircase. All the while, I watched and learned from the three bakers, all of whom had been in the army during World War II. When they saw how eager I was to learn, they took me under their wing and taught me the secrets of the bakery. I began by frying doughnuts and mixing cookie batter. This led to making all sorts of yeast breads—wheat, white, and deli rye. I worked every summer for seven years while in school. I came back to the Sally Ann Food Shop from June through August while putting myself through Bates College in Lewiston, Maine. By the time I graduated, I was a baker. At that point I thought about buying the bakery, but life interceded and I moved on. Fast forward—wherever I went, I knew I could get a job as a baker.

Fermentation fascinated me so much that I studied to become a wine-maker. For five years I immersed myself in another long, slow fermentation. We swapped the Atlantic for the Pacific, settling in Seattle, Washington, while my wife Dolores attended midwifery school. I got a job at Grand Central Baking, a place known for its high-quality baked goods. It was there that I was first introduced to hearth-baked artisan breads and poolishes that utilized similar kinds of long, slow fermentation.

Moving back to Maine in the early 1990s, we settled in Belfast. I baked at a little restaurant there for a year and decided it was time to open my own bakery. We moved into a tiny summer cottage, "not suitable for year-round living," but we managed. In a serendipitous moment, one day a fellow came by, looking for someone who lived in the little house. We got to talking and he told me that he knew of a wood-fired oven in Waldoboro. We made the trip down and met with Harry and Laura Cabot to check out their unused space. It was a tiny basement kitchen, about 600 or 700 square feet, equipped for baking with only a wood-fired oven. The Cabots, who ran the Pine Cone Café on the first floor, agreed to purchase a pair of pizza ovens. I installed soapstone floors in both, so they could serve as hearth-bread-baking ovens. We wrote up a business plan, and that winter we decided it was as good a time as any to launch a new business. We were young and had no idea how much we didn't know. We borrowed money from family and friends, and Bodacious Breads was born.

I quickly perfected my first few bread formulas. Initially we baked and sold wholesale only to the Cabots' restaurant. They used it for their menu and sold loaves retail. Once I had the bakery running smoothly, I sought out a dozen wholesale accounts, mostly co-ops and health food stores within driving distance, from Wiscasset to Belfast. That first summer I baked by myself. Dolores helped with the deliveries. We joke that she was unreliable though. Her deliveries (as a midwife) were much more important than mine! By August I was working seventeen hours a day. From measuring to mixing, kneading to shaping, proofing to baking, I ate, drank, and slept sourdough breads. It was a grueling schedule. I even had a little cot in the corner of the bakery where I rested while the dough rose. One of the store owners in the same downtown block in Waldoboro created a sculpted, papier mâché me, dreaming of breads.

As every baker knows, good bread takes time. There is always something to do today to prep for tomorrow. I recall spending hours hand-pitting olives for the next day's loaves. There was some serious rejoicing when I finally found a good source for already-pitted olives!

In those early days I created fifteen bread formulas. Each of our two ovens could bake 24 to 30 loaves at a time. That meant four to five oven loads a day, producing 96 to 150 breads. By the end of the summer, I hired a woman to help bake, and at the end of the fall, I found someone to help with deliveries. We used our white Ranger pickup with a cap on the back. I remember doing an early morning delivery one day and hitting a deer as it ran across the road. I was devastated. So was the truck, which became abundantly clear as I watched my tire rolling off into the woods. Animals, especially deer, at dawn are a real hazard delivering early morning routes in coastal Maine. One incident can have catastrophic consequences for animal, vehicle, and bread deliveries. The venison, however, was not wasted. It was delicious!

For two years we grew, gradually adding more accounts in the Augusta area. At the close of our second year, we had grown to add several employees and two more ovens. Each oven could bake 60 breads at a time, which bumped our production up to 300 breads a day. We were maxed out on space. Just finding a place to put 300 breads was a problem. The space was brutally hot, with low ceilings and no air-conditioning. One woman baker, when she was in the bakery alone, would even work bare-breasted, it was so hot!

Luckily we found a building near the first bakery. It had previously housed an auto parts store, flea market, and exhaust repair shop and was perfectly situated on busy Route 1, diagonally across from the famous Moody's Diner. We couldn't have asked for a better location! High visibility equals great advertising. Never afraid of drawing attention, we invested in a few gallons of paint and painted the building bright yellow. You couldn't miss us!

We bought the building, which at that point was just a shell, and constructed a fully functional bakery. Our major purchase was a steam-injected deck oven from a company in France . . . for $70,000. The company sent over this extraordinary little old French guy who came in and did everything: plumbing, electrical, masonry, and calibrating. By the time it was complete, the oven weighed twelve tons! Every day he would go across the street to Moody's. The sassy waitresses loved him! He'd hold up his fingers for the number of pieces of toast he wanted with his coffee.

At this point there were few artisan/hearth bread bakers in Maine, which meant little or no competition. I'd put my beret on, carry a basket of bread, and the selling was easy. I liked to say I was "spreading the gospel of good bread." Today, it is very different. I'm happy to say we are fortunate to have many good bakeries, small and large, from Aroostook County to Kittery. I looked for and found my niche—artisan sourdough breads baked on a hearth. From the beginning I recognized and embraced this specialty. I didn't try to do everything but essentially limited the bakery to truly great breads.

We had a basic lineup: peasant, Italian, rye, multigrain, hazelnut, rosemary, walnut, lemon fig, and olive. I added new breads every season, making some types for just a month or two a year. During our second year, around Thanksgiving, I developed an apple bread. I rolled apples in cinnamon, sugar, and spices and incorporated them into the center of each bread. Sounds great, right? Tasted great! The problem was, all the sugar leaked out onto the parchment we had underneath. Thank goodness for the parchment! We had a sticky mess and decided that bread was not going to make a repeat performance ever again!

WHAT'S IN A NAME?

Originally we were known as Bodacious Breads. I loved how voluptuous it sounded. I wanted to have an alliterative name and didn't want brick oven this or bakery that. I wanted a distinctive, memorable name. Bodacious meant something exquisite, admirable, and extraordinary. We were completely happy with it. But a little over three years into our business we got a call from a bakery in Los Angeles. They had trademarked Bodacious Buns and were rolling out a national campaign. They were sending a "request" to cease and desist using the name. Although we were disappointed, we agreed to stop using the name. It was a difficult moment. We had done so much to build our brand, and now we had to shift gears.

Instead of dwelling on the disappointment, we asked customers to help us choose a new name. The prize for coming up with the new name was an annual supply of bread—two loaves a week for an entire year. Astoundingly, we received over 1,200 entries. There were some interesting names in the lot, including "MyGrains from Maine," which we liked but thought would be a headache. Several suggested Crustaceous Breads. Two suggested Borealis Breads. We winnowed the list down to ten and spoke with the staff. Borealis means "from the north," and as one of the northernmost bakeries in the United States, it seemed like the perfect fit. Our new logo was a simple layering of three geometric shapes.

We decided that both of the customers who suggested Borealis should win the same prize. When we called to tell them they had won, we could hear folks screaming and jumping up and down in excitement! Both of the winners are still customers to this day and are very proud of choosing the name. In fact, one of them mentions it every time they come in to the bakery.

What started out feeling like a disaster, we turned around to work in our favor. The name change ended up being an incredible opportunity, as we got a ton of great publicity. I can always tell how long a customer has been buying here. If they refer to us as Bodacious Breads, it's a bright flag that tells me that person has been a customer for over twenty years. I'm pretty proud of that!

A year after becoming Borealis Breads, we opened our second location on busy Route 1 in Wells, Maine. With the expansion we grew to fifty-five employees, over 300 wholesale accounts, and twenty-seven varieties of sourdough bread. We've never been shy about telling our story. Baking up to 3,000 breads a night is a busy business. Each of those loaves is an intensive thirty-plus-hour process. Our high standards and excellent quality are what set us apart from big corporate bakeries. The process from flour to finished loaf earns us a place in our customers' hearts (and bellies). That's the way we can compete in a busy marketplace.

By 2001 we were doing five regular farmers' markets and had a commitment to using Maine grains in at least five varieties of Borealis breads. In addition to wheat, we use many other locally sourced ingredients: Maine potatoes, flint corn, rye, oats, dulse seaweed, maple syrup, honey, and buckwheat, to name just a few.

THE MAINE WHEAT PROJECT

When the bakery was born, I wanted to use as much Maine-grown grain as possible in our breads, but in the late 1990s the quantities just weren't there. When I realized that large-scale grain growing had disappeared from the state, I was alarmed. Our food security depends on being able to grow everything we need. If that was lost, we were on shaky ground, dependent on other people in far-flung places to provide the ingredients we needed at the bakery and at home. I imagined what it would be like to connect all the dots again and nurture this element of sustainable agriculture back to life. There were two things I was certain of: There was much I didn't know, and I couldn't do it alone.

A History of Grains in Maine

Grains have been a part of the Maine foodscape for thousands of years. Long before Europeans arrived in the state, the Algonquian-speaking tribes of Maine were growing and cooking with maize. Beginning in the 1600s European immigrants brought to these shores the grains that were common in their home countries: wheat, rye, oats, barley, and buckwheat. Then, as today, these grains were grown for two purposes: to feed people and livestock. Now Maine's farmers are also growing heritage and ancient grains such as spelt, flint corn, and Red Fife, Magog, Harvard, Maxine, and Warthog wheat.

When I first started looking for flours grown and milled in Maine, I thought it would be a great opportunity to bake some breads made with local flour that would have special appeal for fairgoers. The search for local wheat would send me on a long, winding path. The particulars of my search for flour to use at the fair in the fall of 1995 illustrates the many challenges I needed to overcome.

When purchasing flour for the bakery, I would normally call up one of the bakery or foodservice wholesalers we work with and have the product delivered a couple of days later. It only took a few phone calls to our suppliers for me to realize that asking for locally produced flour was like asking the local fruit farms if they were growing pick-your-own pineapples! Our suppliers had *never* had a request for local flour. As in most cases, if there is no demand for a product, there is no supply either.

At this point I turned to the folks at MOFGA (Maine Organic Farmers and Growers Association). The organization's executive director, Russell Libby, directed me to two farms that were growing wheat for human consumption. The first was Sand Hill Farm in Somerville; the second was King Hill Farm in Penobscot. The farmers were growing a variety of hard red spring wheat called Polk, although both farms were growing the wheat on a very small scale—Sand Hill Farm had an acre or two planted and King Hill had perhaps three acres. Neither farm had enough wheat for me to use.

When I got back in touch with Russell to further pursue local wheat production, he put together a meeting at Thomas College that included farmers, seed specialists, and Cooperative Extension educators. As we explored the availability of small grains for baking, we soon realized that in addition to the lack of wheat, there were no existing processors that could mill enough wheat in the state.

It became clear that reconnecting the farmer, miller, and baker—the holy trinity of bread—would be a long-term project, one that became part of my life's work.

When I met Matt Williams, a farmer and the Cooperative Extension educator, he embraced the possibility of farmers growing more grain. His farm is far north, in Linneus, a town in Aroostook County. Matt was the first person I met who could see my vision for the future of a grain renaissance in Maine. Going forward, Matt got the bit between his teeth and persisted during the times I was crazy busy at the bakery. I knew I wanted to use local wheat, and the people I needed to keep that dream alive, Matt and my wife Dolores, were in my face. That's exactly what had to happen for the idea to stay afloat. Matt was really the engine behind it. His familiarity with the farmers, the seed, the land, and the global connections that had maintained the knowledge of how to grow in our climate were all in the right balance to make it happen. The energy and momentum of the idea began to ping off the right people at the right time and continued to gain speed.

Farmers, educators, scientists, millers, and bakers, local as well as international via the internet, were integral in answering the right questions and keeping the dialogue open to address problems and possibilities we would face. They knew we would need to address which seeds to sow, what soil conditions had to be, how to keep pests and weeds under control, and where the

BREAD WHEATS GROWN IN MAINE

HARD RED SPRING WHEATS
These wheats, not surprisingly, are planted in the spring. Here in Maine they are planted as soon as it is dry enough to get farmers' tractors and equipment onto the fields. Spring wheats can be planted as late as the first week of June. Varieties that have been planted in the last decade in Maine include:

- A.C. Barrie
- A.C. Walton
- Alsen
- Glenn
- Grandin
- Magog
- Polk
- Red Fife
- Roblin

HARD RED WINTER WHEATS
These wheats are planted the last week of August through the middle of September. They grow through the fall, until the colder weather and snow sets in, and then go dormant until spring, when they quickly start growing again. They are typically harvested here in the first three weeks of July. The varieties grown in Maine include:

- Harvard
- Maxine
- Warthog

HARD WHEATS
These are the wheats that are generally used for bread flours. In Maine they have protein contents that vary from 11 to 15 percent. When you bite one of these wheat berries, they are indeed hard and crunchy.

SOFT WHEATS
These are wheats that have a lower protein content and higher starch content; when you bite down on one of these wheat berries, they are soft rather than hard. These wheats are used to produce pastry and cake flours. Because the local demand is primarily for bread flours, I do not know of any Maine farmers growing soft wheats at this time.

RED WHEATS
These wheats have an outer bran layer that is a reddish-brown color.

WHITE WHEAT
These wheats have fewer pigments in the bran layer of the wheat berry, and the whole wheat flours made from them have a milder, less bitter flavor than whole wheat flour made from hard red wheats. Aurora Mills and Farm has grown hard white wheat on an experimental basis.

DURHAM WHEAT
This wheat is most often grown for pasta production. It has a high protein content and a high beta-carotene content, which gives the flour milled from this wheat a slightly yellowish color. Aurora Mills and Farm has grown small quantities of this variety.

SPELT

Spelt is an ancient variety of grain that is related to wheat and was originally cultivated in the Middle East. Like wheat, spelt contains both gluten and gliadin, but in a different ratio. Spelt's higher protein can result in less gluten formation, making it easier for some people with sensitivities to enjoy.

particular numbers that indicate the grains are safe for human consumption and excellent for bread baking. Each step of the way there were challenges, but the idea gained interest, which in turn brought new people in with fresh information and energy that propelled us forward.

Transforming Wheat into Flour

The best test of any bread flour is to bake with it. You can make good bread with good flour, but no matter how good your bread making techniques are, if you are working with poor-quality flour the result will be poor-quality bread. One aspect of quality is based on the gluten protein level of the flour. These proteins provide the crucial characteristics of extensibility and elasticity that allow the bread dough to capture the carbon dioxide being produced by the yeast, which then allows the dough to maintain its shape while rising. The amount of gluten present in any wheat crop is determined by the variety of wheat, weather conditions during the growing season, and, in particular, the amount of available nitrogen in the soil. Good fertilization practices, with effective weed, pest, and disease control, all directly contribute to the production of high-quality wheat flour.

One hundred years ago there was a lot of variability in terms of what was being produced. It certainly helps to have the current testing process, which results in a more consistent commercial product. However, remember to ask the question, how are they making it more consistent? If you're buying conventional flour that has been bleached and bromated, yes, it's very usable. It's consistent, but it's been treated with chemicals that are probably not good for you in the long run. Having local connections and more information about the grains all the way from the farm to the bakery—knowing who grew it, what variety it was, what the conditions were like at the mill—really does help. I have encountered a

lot of variable grain quality over the last twenty years working with local wheat. It makes me a better baker because I have a more thorough understanding about what works, and when it doesn't work, why it might not be working.

Bringing the Aurora to Borealis

That first year Matt Williams planted thirty-two acres of wheat on his fifty-acre farm. This was an incredible leap of faith, devoting more than half his fields to a high-risk experiment. Over the next few growing seasons, several other farms added wheat to their crop rotation. Not everyone was able to produce wheat of acceptable quality. The wheat that did not meet baking standards was either used for animal feed or seed for the following year, or plowed under as a green manure. This loss was also a gain. From these trials we learned what to adjust to improve the quality and characteristics necessary for a usable wheat harvest.

In terms of breaking bread, our holy trinity is made up of farmers, millers, and bakers. Adding others to this mix opened up new horizons. As growers,

ORGANIC VERSUS CONVENTIONAL VERSUS NATURAL FARMING METHODS

ORGANIC

For a farm to be certified organic, fields must be free of pesticides, synthetic fertilizers, genetically modified crops, and other prohibited materials for at least three years before an organic crop can be harvested. Most certifiers will require submission of a farm plan a year ahead, during the winter and early spring for organic crops to be grown the following summer. According to MOFGA, these records must include:

- Seed/seedling/perennials purchase records

- Field activity records (amendments, pesticides, planting dates, manure applications, crop rotation, field histories, etc.)

- Compost production records

- Harvest and sales records (depending on scale and complexity of farm)

Each field must follow the same stringent rules, regardless of what they're growing. This becomes tremendously difficult because each crop affects the next one. Wheat doesn't conflict with other crops, but potatoes do. Potato farmers face catastrophic diseases that are not easily addressed with organic methods. Farmers growing organically nearby could put the crops of their neighbors at risk because some of the weeds that often grow in organic fields can spread damage and disease via wind-blown spores. Longtime farmers can tell, exactly, from which way the wind blows, where trouble in their fields comes from.

CONVENTIONAL

Conventional farming utilizes many different types of naturally occurring and man-made chemicals to help growth, deter pests, and prevent disease. Conventional farmers may or may not use harsh chemicals. In some cases, if one of their crops is prone to blight, a plant disease that can wipe out an entire farm's yield within days of discovery, they have to protect their harvest. They may use organic fertilizers everywhere else; however, that one chemical, vitamin, or mineral that isn't on the organic-approved list prevents them from obtaining organic certification.

NATURAL

Natural farming is a new category. It means that in this field, this year, the crops are grown organically. What was grown last season may have been grown either organically or conventionally with chemicals. Those nonorganic chemicals are possibly still in the soil. If the farmer uses only organic treatments this year, they can use the "naturally-grown" designation.

educators, processors, millers, and bakers learned about the wheat project, each brought a unique perspective that the others needed. Confidence grew, and the wheat project was buzzing all across the state. The greater the interest, the more energy and momentum was generated.

Farmers took the leap, and wheat acreage grew to meet the demand. We went from 32 acres on Matt's farm in 1998 to 100 acres in 2000 to 400 acres in 2018. That's a 1,250 percent increase in twenty years. I knew this expansion of grain production could only continue if everyone involved in the project felt connected to the success. Whether financial, preservational, visionary, or delicious, each piece of the puzzle needed to thrive. At Borealis Breads we certainly have!

The impact of that one inquiry, two decades ago, has changed the trajectory of growing grain in Maine. Remember that. Ask the question. You never know where it could lead in twenty years.

Just like a baby grows longer, then fills out, lengthens again and fills out, the desire for local wheat became the little ball of ice around which a snowball grew as it gained momentum and rolled downhill. Once the inquiry was made to pursue availability of local grains, the supply had to be grown, then the demand followed. This in turn prompted the search for solutions to bring that supply to the hands that demanded it. Therein lay the infrastructure conundrum: How do we connect the dots from seed to slice?

In the late 1990s there was a standing agreement between the United States and Canada that grain could go across the border for processing and come back again without fees. The provision stated that the owner had to stay with the grain until it was processed. During the first few years, farmers were shipping their wheat to Speerville Mill, a grain mill just across the border in New Brunswick. There the wheat was milled into flour, then shipped back to Maine. Some days this "shipping" involved me traveling up to New Brunswick to drop off, wait for, pick up, and deliver the milled flour to the bakery.

Eventually local demand in Canada grew to where Speerville Mill had more custom local milling than they could handle, so they chose to process only local grain from Canada, no US wheat. At that point, Matt Williams was stuck with grain storages full of wheat at his farm in Linneus, Maine, with no way to process. It had no home. So he created one, and Aurora Mills was born. Named specifically to complement Borealis Breads, Aurora Mills, located on his farm,

THE RETURN OF LOCAL

The traditional look of a farm—the meat buildings, the pastures, the livestock—is changing. There are now smaller agricultural entrepreneurs. Statistically there is an increasing number of people deriving part of their income from farming. That economic contribution is important to local communities. If you look at the actual dollars, less than 10 percent of farms produce over 90 percent of the total cash volume. But the other 90 percent are important in many ways.

We all struggle with understanding how food actually makes it to our tables. People used to see it happening in their neighborhood and witnessed the challenges. They could see when the hailstorm crushed the ripe grain in the field. They knew the folks who were working hard; there was a better understanding of the producer.

Today, in a bright, fancy supermarket, most people don't really know how the food gets there. The proximity of relationships to every step in the food supply system is something we all take for granted. Much of the connection has disappeared.

This local food movement *is* a growing segment of society that wants to understand more. The general interest in food and how it's produced gives us back the knowledge base and re-creates those connections. You see it revived in farmers' markets and at community stores. People have the answer to "where did this come from?" People aren't afraid to ask. They still don't want all the grisly details, but we're rebuilding the connections between people and their food, which creates a deeper respect for the risks that farmers take every day.

began the process of re-creating the infrastructure necessary to bring the pieces of the grain puzzle together. The farmers brought their clean wheat to Aurora Mills, where it was stored in silos there until needed. Once milled, the fresh flour went immediately to the bakery to be baked into bread.

The lesson is if you've got a great foodstuff, farm product, or locally processed food that you love and is on your table on a regular basis, don't ever let it go away. It takes twenty times the energy, money, and time to bring it back. So don't lose your food traditions in the first place. They are precious and important, and a part of what makes us who we are.

THE MAINE GRAINS ALLIANCE

In 2007 Michael Scholz, baker and owner of Albion Bread Company, decided he wanted to use more local wheat in his breads. Though there was more local wheat being grown, it had become increasingly difficult to find in quantity because the demand had increased faster than the supply. Michael looked to the north, where Todd Grant had taken over Speerville Mill. They offered a range of sifted flours, but one in particular changed his life. He recounted the moment he opened his first bag of Red Fife, a variety of wheat known for its excellent flavor and low yield. Michael said the aroma was like nothing he had ever baked with before. He immediately tested the new flour. Side by side using another flour and Red Fife, he baked a great bread and an out-of-this-world bread. He felt like he was baking for the first time. This experience led him to realize, once again, that every element of a simple formula has tremendous impact on the final product.

Today there's a nostalgia about bringing old wheat varieties back. Red Fife wheat has a real mystique. It has been identified as a wheat of interest and a Heritage Wheat. Farmers grew Red Fife back in the 1850s and 1860s. To be able to bake with it now feels like we're finally reconnecting those strands of history.

During this same time, Michael and business partner Amber Lambke began working together on the Kneading Conference, a gathering of farmers, grain specialists, professional and amateur baking enthusiasts, wood-fired oven experts, and others passionate about working with grains. Following the Kneading Conference, chockablock full of workshops, an Artisan Bread Fair is held in the same location. These events give attendees an opportunity to share experiences, ask questions of professional bakers, and explore the tools, books, and unending passion that comes from finding your tribe.

There was such a groundswell of enthusiasm in the first years of the Kneading Conference that the Maine Grains Alliance, a 501c3 nonprofit, was born and now runs the event. According to its website, the Maine Grains Alliance mission is "to preserve and promote grain traditions, from earth to table. We provide opportunities to learn and share how best to grow and use grains, using a combination of traditional, innovative, and sustainable techniques. The alliance promotes beneficial uses of grain for good health, food indepen-

A few of the flours ground from grains grown in Maine.

Maine, without reestablishing more of the infrastructure that had been lost. So in 2009 they purchased a historic 1863 building that once was the Somerset County Jail. An old brick stronghold, it has been transformed through extensive renovations into the Somerset Grist Mill. Through the support of the community, loans, and fund-raising efforts, they have raised over a million dollars to bring the mill project to fruition.

Today the mill houses offices for the Maine Grains Alliance and plans to open a café and bakery called The Miller's Table, highlighting extraordinary baked goods made from grain processed on-site. The mill buys wheat, rye, spelt, corn, oats, and heritage grains, and the flours are stone-milled on a four-foot-diameter millstone. They also clean and de-hull grains to process them into berries and flake grains. Increasingly, markets are developing for these products in the craft brewing and distilling industries.

In addition the Maine Grains Alliance is currently restoring the supply of plantable seed for several kinds of rare and heritage ryes and wheats. As a result of careful growth, collection, and restoration, the Maine Grains Alliance now maintains the Western Hemisphere's most extensive stock of a rare Estonian wheat called Sirvinta.

dence, and purposeful jobs within viable communities. The alliance connects people and supports the economic, environmental, and nutritional importance for establishing regional grain economies."

Michael and Amber knew there was only so far they could go to encourage the growth of the grain economy in Skowhegan, and farther afield in

THE BAKER'S WAY

The Path to Great Bread

✕

*There is a rhythm to sourdough bread making that defies the
pell-mell of our daily lives and compels one to slow down and take
notice of small things: the gritty feel of whole wheat flour, a whiff
of sourdough tang, the crackling sound of a bread crust cooling
just after it is pulled from the oven . . . all of these and more
will delight your senses as you develop your bread baking skills.*

UNDERSTANDING THE RECIPES

A BREAD RECIPE IS FAR MORE THAN just a list of ingredients
and a few lines of instruction as to how to assemble them. A recipe is a map
of the relationship between ingredients, and baker's percentages are the key to
understanding that map. As you can see in the sample below, the recipes in this
book are presented in three formats: metric units (grams), U.S. customary units
(ounces), and, in a few cases, baker's percentage.

I have also chosen to include volumetric measurements such as cups and
tablespoons; however, they are not very accurate and do little to illustrate the
ratios between ingredients. For example, if you scoop out bread flour from a

container, the weight can vary considerably depending on how much flour is packed into the measuring cup. Measuring by volume does not take this into account, nor does it allow for the density of the ingredients you are measuring. Flours have different densities—imagine a cup of feathers beside a cup of pebbles. Of course they won't be the same weight. A cup of wheat flour does not weigh the same as a cup of buckwheat flour. In fact, even the same type of flour can have different densities depending on how it was milled. Measuring by weight allows the baker to utilize a standardized measurement that works equally well for wet and dry ingredients and for ingredients of different densities.

If you really want to ramp up your bread baking game, you will want to make one other change. Most folks still use ounces and pounds when weighing out ingredients; fortunately, most digital scales today allow you to weigh your ingredients using the precision of grams instead. I strongly recommend measuring your ingredients by weight in grams, as it is far more accurate.

Baker's Percentages

Using baker's percentages is a method of expressing a recipe as a set of ratios. The total amount of flour used in the recipe, including the flour in the sourdough starter, is given a value of 100 percent. All the other ingredients are expressed as a percentage of the total flour used in the recipe. Once you know the total flour weight, you can divide the weight of any ingredient into the total flour weight to determine the baker's percentage, or the ratio between the two ingredients.

FIGURE OUT YOUR BREAD MAKING SCHEDULE

Great bread is not something hastily made. The recipes in this book take time. A straight yeasted bread can be made in three to four hours from start to finish, but the resulting loaf is one whose flavors are simple and one dimensional. Slow fermentations greatly enhance a bread's flavor. While the actual time spent mixing, kneading, and shaping will take only fifteen to twenty minutes, the elapsed time from when you first feed the sourdough starter to when the bread comes out of the oven will be anywhere from eighteen to thirty-six hours. The sourdough starters used in these recipes, once fed, take anywhere from four to sixteen hours to develop before they can be used to leaven your bread. With a little thought and experience, you will be able to develop baking routines that are suited to your personal schedule.

Here are two time lines to serve as a guide for planning your bread baking process.

		WHITE SOURDOUGH STARTER						100% HYDRATION		
TIME	7:00 PM	7 PM– 7 AM	7 AM– 7:15 AM	7:15 AM– 7:45 AM	7:45 AM– 8 AM	8 AM– 11 AM	11:00 AM	11 AM– 2 PM	2:15 PM– 3 PM
ACTIVITY	MIX STARTER	FERMENT STARTER	MIX DOUGH	REST DOUGH	ADD SALT KNEAD DOUGH	FIRST RISE	SHAPE BREAD	SECOND RISE	BAKE BREAD

		WHOLE WHEAT SOURDOUGH STARTER						60% HYDRATION		
TIME	11:00 PM	7 PM– 7 AM	7 AM– 7:15 AM	7:15 AM– 7:45 AM	7:45 AM– 8 AM	8 AM– 10:30 AM	10:30 AM	11 AM–1 PM	1 PM– 1:45 PM
ACTIVITY	MIX STARTER	FERMENT STARTER	MIX DOUGH	REST DOUGH	ADD SALT KNEAD DOUGH	FIRST RISE		SHAPE BREAD	SECOND RISE	BAKE BREAD

GATHER YOUR INGREDIENTS AND BAKING GEAR

While your sourdough starter is growing, you will have ample time to prepare for baking. A little organization in the kitchen goes a long way to ensuring a smooth bread baking day. Gather up everything you will need and have it close at hand. This is the time to make sure you have all the ingredients called for in the recipe. It's better to know you are out of salt before you mix up your dough, rather than after.

PREP THE INGREDIENTS

A number of the recipes in this book require some preparatory kitchen work. Whether it involves toasting nuts or cooking up a corn mash, these tasks can be accomplished between the time you mix your sourdough starter and the time you mix your dough. If any ingredients need to be cooked, it's important that you also allow enough time for them to cool to room temperature. Adding a hot mash to the mix will send dough temperatures soaring and compromise the quality of the bread you are creating.

MEASURE THE INGREDIENTS

In the bakery, we measure all ingredients by weight. This is both accurate and fast, and I find the same is true when I bake at home. I strongly recommend measuring ingredients by weight in grams, as this is the easiest and most accurate method. I have included volumetric measurements such as cups and tablespoons for those who do not have access to a scale; however, as mentioned, volumetric measurements are not very accurate or consistent.

MIX THE DOUGH

This is where the magic of bread begins. Mixing the dough will evenly distribute the ingredients, initiate the fermentation, and develop the gluten that will provide the essential extensibility and elasticity for the bread.

Mixing the dough to the proper temperature is very important in order to get the fermentation off to a strong start. The dough temperature when fully mixed and kneaded should be between 70°F and 82°F. Mix cooler than this and the dough will ferment very slowly. Mix warmer and it will rise too quickly, easily over-proof, and lack the depth of flavor that results from a slower fermentation.

Many of the recipes in this book utilize a technique known as autolyse, a methodology first developed by Professor Raymond Calvel, a renowned French scientist who extensively researched ways to improve bread quality. It is simply a rest period that allows the flour to absorb water and start aligning the strands of gluten.

If the bread formula utilizes a high-hydration starter containing a significant portion of the water that is found in the final dough, only the flour, water, and

THE WINDOWPANE TEST

Take a small piece of dough about the size of a golf ball and see how far you can stretch it between two hands. If you can gently pull it out to the point that it becomes a pane of translucent, almost transparent dough, then the gluten is well developed. If the dough shreds before it becomes a translucent pane, then it needs to be kneaded more. The windowpane test works best on doughs that contain 100 per-cent white bread flour. Doughs made with whole wheat or other grains that contain little or no gluten, such as corn, rye, and barley, can still be tested using the windowpane method, but will not stretch out quite as far or as thin before they start to rip. Oats or ingredients that tend to break up the strands of gluten will have less extensibility, and the dough will shred before you can see through it.

sourdough starter are mixed together. All other ingredients: salt, nuts, fruits, seeds, corn mash, and whole grains are added after the autolyse period. The results of this technique allow the bread to be kneaded less, and promote better flavor and bread volume.

KNEAD/STRETCH

After the autolyse rest period, the bread must be kneaded to continue the gluten development. If the dough hydration is under 70 percent, take the dough out of the bowl and place it on a work surface that has no flour on it. Start to knead by taking the piece of dough and folding it in half, then pushing it down and away from you. Bring the bread back to its original position close to you and turn it 90 degrees. Repeat the fold and push steps until the gluten has fully developed.

To test if your bread has been kneaded enough, you can perform what is known as the "windowpane test." As you knead you will feel the dough tightening up; this is the elasticity of the gluten expressing itself. If the dough tightens up so much that the smooth outer surface of the dough starts to shred, then it is time to stop kneading and let it rest for a few minutes. This will allow the dough to relax enough so that you can continue kneading without tearing it. Breads with a hydration of over 70 percent, which are difficult to knead without incorporating a lot of flour, will require one or more stretch and folds to help develop the gluten and make a wet dough easier to handle.

FIRST RISE

The first rise, or the bulk fermentation, as we say in the trade, plays a large role in the overall quality of the bread. In most cases the dough should rest in a bowl covered with a damp cloth. The time of the first rise depends on the temperature of your ingredients and the room where you are baking. In my kitchen the first rise usually takes about an hour.

SHAPING THE BREAD

Bread shaping is one of those skills that develops over time. Each dough has its own texture and appearance. The amount of hydration, stickiness of the dough, and any add-ins will all affect the ease with which a dough can be shaped. At the bakery, each bread has its own distinctive shape.

SECOND PROOF (RISE)

After the bread is shaped, it will go though its last fermentation prior to being baked. Typically most breads almost double in size during this period. How to judge when a bread is ready to bake is one of the most common questions I get when I am teaching baking classes. To ascertain whether a bread is ready to pop in the oven, you can employ the poke test. Simply put, you poke the bread. If the bread still feels dense and the indentation you have created springs back quickly, leaving little or no trace, then the bread is under-proofed and needs to rise longer. If the indentation barely springs back, doesn't spring back at all, or even deflates the dough, then the bread is over-proofed. If you poke the bread and it springs back slowly and leaves a small indentation, then it is ready to be baked. As you handle bread dough and work with your favorite recipes over and over again, you will develop a "feel" for the bread that includes visual and tactile cues typical for the specific breads you are making.

SCORING THE BREAD

Scoring bread is done for both practical and aesthetic reasons. Scoring should be done just before the bread is put into the oven. The best tool for scoring is a lamé, which is basically a handle of some sort to which you attach a double-sided razor blade. In a pinch, when I have razor blades but have forgotten to bring the metal handle to hold them, I have found that a wooden coffee stirrer makes an admirable substitute for the razor holder. The advantage of the lamé is that it is easily manipulated and can be used to make all kinds of cuts, straight or curved, deep or shallow. If you don't have a lamé, then an alternative available in most kitchens would be a serrated knife. The serrated knife is best used for making straight cuts.

When the bread is first put into the oven, it rises very quickly, and the slashes act as expansion joints, allowing it to rise to its fullest volume. Scoring also provides the baker the opportunity to apply some artistic finishing touches that will create a loaf with great visual appeal. People eat with their eyes first, as we say at the bakery, so a well-proofed, well-scored loaf is one that enhances our desire for that scrumptious-looking bread.

Scoring needs to be done resolutely and quickly. If you score slowly, the slashes will be irregular and the blade will keep snagging on the bread.

BAKING YOUR BREAD

There are many variables to consider as you get ready to bake. First, give some thought to the oven you will be baking in. Does the temperature dial for the oven accurately register the true temperature? Does the oven bake evenly? Is it hotter on the top than the bottom? Will you need to turn the bread halfway through the bake to ensure it bakes evenly? If your oven has a convection option, make sure it is turned *off* when baking bread. The air movement when a convection fan is running will accelerate crust formation, producing a leathery unpleasant crust, and reduce bread volume.

Most of the breads in this book are not pan breads and should be baked on a sheet pan or baking stone. Prior to loading the bread into the oven, steam needs to be introduced. If baking on a baking stone, one hour prior to baking, place your stone on the center oven shelf and, using the non-convection mode, preheat the oven to 500°F. If baking on a sheet pan, preheat the oven 20 minutes prior to the bake. Ten minutes prior to baking, place a sheet pan (one with sides) on the bottom shelf of the oven and fill with 1½ cups boiling water. Just prior to baking the breads, add more boiling water to the sheet pan. Use caution, as the steam that escapes when the oven door is opened can easily cause burns. Open the oven carefully, keeping your face and hands out of the billowing cloud of steam.

If using a baking stone, transfer the breads seam down to a peel that has been lightly dusted with semolina or cornmeal and immediately peel the breads onto the baking stone. If using a sheet pan, place the pan with the breads on it directly into the oven on the middle shelf. Bake for 30 to 35 minutes. Most home ovens bake unevenly, so you may need to turn the breads after 20 minutes. When fully baked, remove the breads from the oven and place on a cooling rack.

Test for Doneness

For most folks, a glance at the color of the bread and a quick tap on the bottom of the loaf that produces a hollow sound are all the indications they need to judge whether the bread is ready to come out of the oven. The classic test for doneness is that tap on the bottom of the bread: If it sounds hollow, it is done; if it sounds dull, then the bread needs more baking time. A less subjective test is to measure the internal temperature of the bread.

CREATING A SOURDOUGH STARTER

CREATING YOUR OWN SOURDOUGH STARTER takes some time but is not difficult to do. You can make a starter using only a single type of flour, such as white bread flour, whole rye flour, or whole wheat flour, or you can use a blend, as I have in the formula below. While using nonorganic flour may work for you, the grains ground for that flour most likely have been treated with fungicides that can kill the wild yeast found on the grain. Organic flours provide a much better base for creating a starter from scratch. Rye flour ferments very easily, and for that reason I have included a small portion as a booster in this starter formula.

IMPORTANT NOTE ABOUT WATER

If you are on town/public water or are using a household water softening system, I recommend using bottled spring water to mix your starters. The chemicals used to treat municipal water supplies and to soften water will inhibit or totally stop the activity of the yeast and bacteria on which you are relying to grow your natural organic starter.

Starter	INGREDIENT	WEIGHT	BAKER'S %
	WATER (80°F TO 90°F)	100 GRAMS	100
	ORGANIC BREAD FLOUR	85 GRAMS	85
	ORGANIC WHOLE RYE FLOUR	15 GRAMS	15
	TOTAL FLOUR	100 GRAMS	100
	TOTAL WEIGHT	200 GRAMS	

Starter Refresh	INGREDIENT	WEIGHT	BAKER'S %
	WATER (80°F TO 90°F)	80 GRAMS	100
	ORGANIC BREAD FLOUR	80 GRAMS	100
	STARTER	40 GRAMS	40

Mix the ingredients together until they form a thick batter with no lumps. The batter temperature should ideally be between 75°F and 80°F. Place the batter in a transparent container, such as a glass bowl or a wide-mouthed glass mason jar, that will allow you to observe the fermentation activity. Keep the container covered. The container should be no more than one-third full to allow for the mixture to rise as it ferments.

Set the starter in a spot where the temperature will remain between 75°F and 80°F. The process should begin spontaneously over the next couple of days. It will start slowly, and you will see just a few fermentation bubbles rising to the top of the starter. As the yeast population increases, the fermentation activity will increase. Leave it undisturbed until the fermentation has created froth on the top of the starter and it is bubbly throughout. Test this starter by scooping out a dollop and placing it in a small bowl of water: If it floats, the starter is ready to be fed; if it sinks, let the starter continue to ferment until it passes this "float test."

Once the starter has passed the float test, it is time to refresh the starter. In a bowl mix together the ingredients noted above; again the temp should be between 75°F and 80°F. Again place the starter in a clear container, cover, and let sit. The excess starter from the first mix can be discarded or used to make sourdough pancakes. The refreshed starter will ferment much more quickly and should be fully active within 12 to 15 hours if kept between 70°F and 80°F. Use the float test to determine if the starter is ready to be used for baking.

You have now created a living, symbiotic community of yeast and bacteria that can accomplish amazing feats of fermentation. At this point people often give their starters a name. While my starters do not have names, I do call them my babies.

To create scrumptious breads that will amaze your family and friends, you will need to treat your living, growing starter with care and consideration to ensure it will thrive. When I began baking in Maine, I received my first starter from my friend Boo Hubbard, who in turn had gotten it from her grandmother. That starter is now over sixty years old! You can keep your starter living indefinitely if you continue to strengthen and feed it. The best way to do this is to continue baking. Continuing to feed, ferment, and divide the starter will ensure it continues to thrive.

CARE, FEEDING, AND BAKING SCHEDULE

Once your starter is well established, it's time to incorporate it into your baking schedule. If you are not using the starter every day or two, it can be stored in the refrigerator for a week or two, possibly more. To refrigerate, place the starter in a glass jar no more than one-third full and cover. We use a quart-size mason jar with a lid.

GET READY FOR BAKING DAY

One of the delightful things about sourdough baking is that it *does* take time and planning. The first step is refreshing the starter. Remove the jar of chilled starter from the refrigerator and place on the counter in an undisturbed place to come to room temperature, ideally a few hours before you're going to bake. Now it's time to feed those little bubbles. Weigh the starter per the recipe and

place in a medium bowl. Add an equal amount of flour and water to the starter by weight. If you're using volume measurements, measure the starter and add an equal volume of water and one and one-half times as much flour. For instance, if you're starting with 1 cup starter, add 1 cup slightly warm water and 1½ cups flour. Stir gently to combine. Divide this new starter in half into two clear, quart-size glass jars—it will need space as it begins to wake up and grow. Mark the level of the mixture on the jars.

If you plan to bake only a single batch of bread, cover one of the jars with a metal lid and return it to the refrigerator to save for another day. Place the jar of starter you plan to use out on the counter in an area between 70°F and 80°F where it will be undisturbed. Cover with a paper towel. Use an elastic or piece of string to affix the paper towel over the top of the jar. Allow the starter to bubble and grow for 4 to 6 hours, or until it has doubled in size. Now you're ready to bake! Use this starter in the recipes that follow. Remember, starters are meant to be shared.

THE BREADS

IN THE BEGINNING . . .

I open with these first five breads—Italian, French Peasant, Olive, Portuguese Corn, and Rosemary Hazelnut—because they were the first breads we offered to our customers when we opened for business in June 1993. In those exuberant days, we delivered our hand-shaped breads naked—no sliced breads and no packaging. Our retail customers displayed the breads in baskets that we provided. Those unabashed loaves quickly enthralled shoppers in the mid-coast area, and within months I was hiring my first employees to keep up with the demand. It would be a few years later that I would start exploring the potential for locally grown grains, so it is not surprising that I named the first breads with a nod to the European bread baking traditions that inspired my craft. If I were to name them today, they would bear names that would remark on their local provenance here in Maine.

Italian Bread

YIELDS 2 LOAVES

If you don't have a lot of experience with bread baking, this is a great recipe to start with. Its simplicity allows you to focus on the interplay of ingredients, how the gluten develops, and the transition from a shaggy ball of dough to a silky-smooth dough with great elasticity. This bread for me evokes memories of the Italian bakeries in Boston's North End and in Revere—chock-full of crusty, hand-shaped loaves—that beguiled me on our family trips into Boston or over to Revere Beach.

Recipe

Sourdough Starter

	GRAMS	OUNCES	VOLUME
FLOUR	112	4.0	⅔ CUP + 1 TBSP
WATER	112	4.0	½ CUP
WHITE SOURDOUGH MOTHER	34	1.2	⅛ CUP
TOTAL	258	9.2	

Dough

	GRAMS	OUNCES	VOLUME	BAKERS %
BREAD FLOUR	700	24.7	4½ CUPS	100.0%
SOURDOUGH STARTER	210	7.4	¾ CUP + 2 TBSP	30.0%
WATER	434	15.3	2½ CUPS + 2 TBSP	62.0%
SALT	16	0.6	SCANT TBSP	2.3%
TOTAL	1,360	48		

Procedure

MIX THE SOURDOUGH STARTER

Measure the ingredients for the sourdough starter into a bowl, and with a spatula or whisk mix vigorously until the ingredients have been uniformly mixed together with no lumps remaining. The sourdough temperature when mixed should be between 70°F and 80°F. Let this mixture ferment until fully developed, approximately 10 to 12 hours.

MEASURE AND MIX THE DOUGH

Measure out the salt and set aside. Measure into a large bowl the bread flour, sourdough starter, and water. Using a spatula or plastic scraper, mix the ingredients together until the flour is just evenly incorporated into a ball of dough. The dough temperature should be between 70°F and 80°F. Make sure to save the leftover sourdough starter to use as a sourdough mother in later bakes!

REST AND ADD SALT
Cover the bowl with a damp cloth and let the dough rest for 30 minutes. After the dough has rested, leave the dough in the bowl and sprinkle half the salt over the dough, then flip it over and sprinkle the rest of the salt over the other side. Leaving the dough in the bowl, gently knead the salt into the dough until it is fully incorporated.

KNEAD
Turn the dough out onto a lightly floured work surface and knead until the gluten is fully developed. As you knead, you may need to dust your work surface with flour occasionally to stop the dough from sticking. If the dough tightens up so that it is not easily kneaded without shredding the surface of the dough, cover it with the mixing bowl and let it rest for 3 to 5 minutes, during which time the dough will relax and become workable again. Continue kneading until the dough is supple and smooth.

FIRST RISE
Place the dough back in the bowl and cover the bowl with a damp cloth. Let the dough rise for 45 minutes. Again remove it from the bowl, gently stretch and fold the dough, then place it back in the bowl. Continue to let the dough rise until fully proofed, using the poke test to ascertain when to shape the dough.

PORTION AND SHAPE
Remove the dough from the bowl and divide into two equal pieces, each weighing 1 pound, 8 ounces. Loosely pre-shape the pieces into rounds, cover with a damp cloth, and let rest for 5 minutes. Shape each piece into a torpedo with tapered ends. Place the shaped breads seam down on a sheet pan that has been dusted with cornmeal or semolina, or seam up on a linen bread couche that has been dusted with flour (leave a fold of the linen between the two breads to separate them).

SECOND RISE AND SCORE
Cover the breads with a damp cloth and let rise in a draft-free area. Employ the poke test to judge when to bake the breads. If the breads are proofing in a linen

bread couche, they will need to be transferred seam down to another sheet pan that has been dusted with semolina or cornmeal. If proofed on a sheet pan, they may stay on that pan and be loaded directly into the oven.

Just before the breads are to be loaded into the oven, score using a bread lamé. Hold the razor at a 45-degree angle and give each bread three evenly spaced diagonal scores on the top of the loaf.

BAKE

The breads may be baked on a baking stone or on a sheet pan. If baking on a baking stone, 1 hour prior to baking, place your stone on the center oven shelf and, using the non-convection mode, preheat the oven to 500°F. If baking on a sheet pan, preheat the oven 20 minutes prior to the bake. Ten minutes prior to baking, place a sheet pan (one with sides) on the bottom shelf of the oven and fill with 1½ cups boiling water. Just prior to baking the breads, add more boiling water to the sheet pan. If using a baking stone, transfer the breads seam down to a peel that has been lightly dusted with semolina or cornmeal and immediately peel the breads onto the baking stone. If using a sheet pan, place the pan with the breads on it directly into the oven on the middle shelf.

Bake for 30 to 35 minutes. Most home ovens bake unevenly, so you may need to turn the breads after 20 minutes. When fully baked, remove the breads from the oven and place on a cooling rack.

FRENCH PEASANT BREAD

YIELDS 2 LOAVES

Consistently one of our best sellers, this bread's hallmark is its versatility—as a sandwich bread, as a toasting bread, at the dinner table, and as an accompaniment for any number of foods. At the bakery, we now make it in many forms: a round boule, a long loaf, and a sliced sandwich loaf. When we started, we sold it almost exclusively as a round, proofed in a willow basket with a star slash on top. That is how I present it here.

Recipe

Sourdough Starter

	GRAMS	OUNCES	VOLUME
FLOUR	110	3.9	¾ CUP
WATER	110	3.9	½ CUP
WHITE SOURDOUGH MOTHER	33	1.2	⅛ CUP
TOTAL	252	9	

Dough

	GRAMS	OUNCES	VOLUME
BREAD FLOUR	577	20.4	3¾ CUPS + 1 TBSP
WHOLE WHEAT FLOUR	112	4.0	¾ CUP
SOURDOUGH STARTER	207	7.3	¾ CUP + 3 TBSP
WATER	448	15.8	2 CUPS + 2 TSP
SALT	16	0.6	1 TBSP
TOTAL	1,360	48.1	

Procedure

MIX THE SOURDOUGH STARTER

Measure the ingredients for the sourdough starter into a bowl, and with a spatula or whisk mix vigorously until the ingredients have been uniformly mixed together with no lumps remaining. The sourdough temperature when mixed should be between 75°F and 80°F. Let this mixture ferment until fully developed, approximately 10 to 12 hours.

MEASURE AND MIX THE DOUGH

Measure out the salt and set aside. Measure into a large bowl the bread flours, sourdough starter, and water. Using a spatula or plastic scraper, mix the ingredients together until the flour is just evenly incorporated into a ball of dough. The dough temperature should be between 70°F and 80°F. Make sure to save the leftover sourdough starter to use as a sourdough mother in later bakes!

REST AND ADD SALT
Cover the bowl with a damp cloth and let the dough rest for 30 minutes. After the dough has rested, leave the dough in the bowl and sprinkle half the salt over the dough, then flip it over and sprinkle the rest of the salt over the other side. Leaving the dough in the bowl, gently knead the salt into the dough until it is fully incorporated.

KNEAD
Turn the dough out onto a lightly floured work surface and knead until the gluten is fully developed. As you knead, you may need to dust your work surface with flour occasionally to stop the dough from sticking. If the dough tightens up so that it is not easily kneaded without shredding the surface of the dough, cover it with the mixing bowl and let it rest for 3 to 5 minutes, during which time the dough will relax and become workable again. Continue kneading until the dough is supple and smooth.

FIRST RISE
Place the dough back in the bowl and cover the bowl with a damp cloth. Let the dough rise for 45 minutes. Again remove it from the bowl, gently stretch and fold the dough, then place it back in the bowl. Continue to let the dough rise until fully proofed, using the poke test to ascertain when to shape the dough.

PORTION AND SHAPE
Remove the dough from the bowl and divide into two equal pieces, each weighing 1 pound, 8 ounces. Shape each piece into a round. Place the shaped breads seam down on a sheet pan that has been dusted with cornmeal or semolina, or seam up in proofing baskets that have been dusted with flour.

SECOND RISE AND SCORE
Cover the breads with a damp cloth and let rise in a draft-free area. Employ the poke test to judge when to bake the breads. If the breads are proofing in baskets, they will need to be transferred seam down to another sheet pan that has been dusted with semolina or cornmeal. If proofed on a sheet pan, they may stay on that pan and be loaded directly into the oven.

Just before the breads are to be loaded into the oven, slash the top of each loaf using a bread lamé. Hold the razor at a 90-degree angle and give each bread two slashes that form an X across the top and one slash across the middle of the X. The slashes intersect at the center of the bread, forming an asterisk-like design. The spaces between the six lines radiating from the center should be equal in size.

BAKE

The breads may be baked on a baking stone or on a sheet pan. If baking on a baking stone, 1 hour prior to baking, place your stone on the center oven rack and, using the non-convection mode, preheat the oven to 500°F. If baking on a sheet pan, preheat the oven 20 minutes prior to the bake. Ten minutes prior to baking, place a sheet pan (one with sides) on the bottom shelf of the oven and fill with 1½ cups boiling water. Just prior to baking the breads, add more boiling water to the sheet pan so there is at least ½ inch of water in the pan. If using a baking stone, transfer the breads seam down onto a peel that has been lightly dusted with semolina or cornmeal and immediately peel the breads onto the baking stone. If using a sheet pan, place the pan with the breads on it directly into the oven on the middle shelf.

Bake for 30 to 35 minutes. Most home ovens bake unevenly, so you may need to turn the breads after 20 minutes. When fully baked, remove the breads from the oven and place on a cooling rack.

Olive Bread

YIELDS 2 LOAVES

Whether in the form of olive oil, olivada, or just plain olives, the fruit of the European olive tree seems to have a natural affinity with bread. My original formula for this bread called for kalamata olives, known for their robust fruity flavor. When I first went to source the olives for this bread, the only ones I could find at the time were unpitted olives. Unpitted kalamatas in bread are a recipe for dental disaster, so at the end of my fifteen-hour days that first summer, I would sit exhausted on the receiving dock at the back of the bakery overlooking the Medomak River and pit five to six pounds of olives in preparation for the next day's mix. Sometime during our second year I finally found pitted olives, and hallelujah, the daily pitting ordeal was over! The pitting process is not perfect, so to this day we still hand-squeeze each olive to ensure that no pits remain. While kalamatas work well in this recipe, any olive will do, and I often mix several varieties into the bread.

Recipe

Sourdough Starter	GRAMS	OUNCES	VOLUME
FLOUR	120	4.2	¾ CUP + 2 TSP
WATER	120	4.2	½ CUP + 1 TBSP
WHITE SOURDOUGH MOTHER	36	1.3	⅛ CUP + 1 TSP
TOTAL	276	9.7	

Dough	GRAMS	OUNCES	VOLUME
BREAD FLOUR	566	20.0	3¾ CUPS
SOURDOUGH STARTER	226	8.0	1 CUP
WATER	396	14.0	1¾ CUPS + 1 TBSP
OLIVES, PITTED	158	5.6	1 CUP
SALT	14	0.5	1 TBSP
TOTAL	1,360	48.1	

Procedure

MIX THE SOURDOUGH STARTER

Measure the ingredients for the sourdough starter into a bowl, and with a spatula or whisk mix vigorously until the ingredients have been uniformly mixed together with no lumps remaining. The sourdough temperature when mixed should be between 75°F and 80°F. Let this mixture ferment until fully developed, approximately 10 to 12 hours.

MEASURE AND MIX THE DOUGH
Measure out the salt and olives and set aside. Measure into a large bowl the bread flour, sourdough starter, and water. Using a spatula or plastic scraper, mix the ingredients together until the flour is just evenly incorporated into a ball of dough. The dough temperature should be between 70°F and 80°F. Make sure to save the leftover sourdough starter to use as a sourdough mother in later bakes!

REST AND ADD SALT
Cover the bowl with a damp cloth and let the dough rest for 30 minutes. After the dough has rested, leave the dough in the bowl and sprinkle half the salt over the dough, then flip it over and sprinkle the rest of the salt over the other side. Leaving the dough in the bowl, gently knead until the salt is fully incorporated.

KNEAD AND ADD OLIVES
Turn the dough out onto a lightly floured work surface and knead until the gluten is fully developed. As you knead, you may need to dust your work surface with flour occasionally to stop the dough from sticking. If the dough tightens up so that it is not easily kneaded without shredding the surface of the dough, cover it with the mixing bowl and let it rest for 3 to 5 minutes, during which time the dough will relax and become workable again. Continue kneading until the dough is supple and smooth.

Cover the dough with the mixing bowl and let it relax for 5 minutes. Flatten the dough out and press the olives into both sides of the dough, then fold the dough up and knead it a couple of turns to evenly distribute the olives.

FIRST RISE
Place the dough back in the bowl and cover the bowl with a damp cloth. Let the dough rise for 45 minutes. Again remove it from the bowl, gently stretch and fold the dough, then place it back in the bowl. Continue to let the dough rise until fully proofed, using the poke test to ascertain when to shape the dough.

PORTION AND SHAPE
Remove the dough from the bowl and divide into two equal pieces, each weighing 1 pound, 8 ounces. Fold each piece so it is 4 inches wide and at least 10

inches long, and roll up like a round hay bale. Heavily dust the last 2 inches of the roll with flour and do not seal the seam. Place the shaped breads seam down on a sheet pan that has been dusted with cornmeal or semolina, or on a linen bread couche that has been dusted with bread or rice flour (leave a fold of the linen between the two breads to separate them).

SECOND RISE

Cover the breads with a damp cloth and let rise in a draft-free area. Employ the poke test to judge when to bake the breads. If the breads are proofing on a linen bread couche, they will need to be transferred seam up to another sheet pan or to a peel that has been dusted with semolina or cornmeal. If proofed on a sheet pan, pick up the loaves and place on the sheet pan seam up after applying more cornmeal or semolina to the pan. Lift the seam up so that 1 to 1½ inches of dough no longer adheres to the dough underneath it.

BAKE

The breads may be baked on a baking stone or on a sheet pan. If baking on a baking stone, 1 hour prior to baking, place your stone on the center oven shelf and, using the non-convection mode, preheat the oven to 500°F. If baking on a sheet pan, preheat the oven 20 minutes prior to the bake. Ten minutes prior to baking, place a sheet pan (one with sides) on the bottom shelf of the oven and fill with 1½ cups boiling water. Just prior to baking the breads, add more boiling water to the sheet pan. If using a baking stone, transfer the breads seam down to a peel that has been lightly dusted with semolina or cornmeal and immediately peel the breads onto the baking stone. If using a sheet pan, place the pan with the breads on it directly into the oven on the middle shelf.

Bake for 30 to 35 minutes. Most home ovens bake unevenly, so you may need to turn the breads after 20 minutes. When fully baked, remove the breads from the oven and place on a cooling rack.

PORTUGUESE CORN BREAD

YIELDS 2 LOAVES

My grandfather Mariano Amaral was born in the Azores and immigrated to the states as a young man. For many years he was a baker and cook at Pieroni's Seafood Grill, a well-known restaurant on Washington Street in downtown Boston. His baking career ended long before mine started, so unfortunately we never talked about baking or shared recipes. Years later, while I was the winemaker at Sakonnet Vineyards, I came across pau de milho, a yeasted corn bread sold at the Portuguese bakeries in Fall River, Massachusetts. In memory of Mariano I decided to create my own version when I started Borealis Breads. During my sojourn at Sakonnet Vineyards, I lived a stone's throw from Gray's Gristmill in Westport, Massachusetts, where Tim the miller ground a locally grown white cap Indian flint corn into Johnny cake meal. I used that cornmeal for my home bread baking back then, and will always remember the outstanding flavor of that heritage flint cornmeal. Fortunately, today you can find Maine-grown heritage flint cornmeal in many food co-ops, and it adds a truly special flavor to this bread.

Recipe

Sourdough Starter

Sourdough Starter	GRAMS	OUNCES	VOLUME
FLOUR	74	2.6	½ CUP
WATER	74	2.6	⅓ CUP + 1 TSP
WHITE SOURDOUGH MOTHER	19	0.7	
TOTAL	167	5.9	

Prep	GRAMS	OUNCES	VOLUME
FLINT CORNMEAL	70	2.5	⅔ CUP + 1 TBSP
WATER	279	9.8	1¾ CUPS + 1 TBSP
TOTAL	349	12.3	

Dough	GRAMS	OUNCES	VOLUME
BREAD FLOUR	617	21.8	4 CUPS + 1 TBSP
SOURDOUGH STARTER	185	6.5	¾ CUP + 1 TBSP
WATER	247	8.7	1⅛ CUPS
CORN MASH	295	10.4	1¼ CUPS
SALT	16	0.6	1 TBSP
TOTAL	1,360	48	

Procedure

MIX THE SOURDOUGH STARTER

Measure the ingredients for the sourdough starter into a bowl, and with a spatula or whisk mix vigorously until the ingredients have been uniformly mixed together with no lumps remaining. The sourdough temperature when mixed should be between 72°F and 80°F. Let this mixture ferment until fully developed, approximately 10 to 12 hours.

PREP

The cornmeal used in this recipe needs to be cooked prior to adding it to the dough. Place the cornmeal and water in a heavy-bottomed saucepan and let simmer slowly at a very low heat, stirring every 5 minutes to ensure it does not stick to the bottom of the pan. When done, the corn mash should be soft and not gritty. It's a good idea to taste it to be sure the consistency is correct. Remove from the heat and let cool to room temperature before adding to the dough.

MEASURE AND MIX THE DOUGH

Measure out the salt and set aside. Measure into a large bowl the bread flour, sourdough starter, water, and corn mash. Using a spatula or plastic scraper, mix the ingredients together until evenly incorporated into a ball of dough. The dough temperature should be between 70°F and 80°F. Make sure to save the leftover sourdough starter to use as a sourdough mother in later bakes!

REST AND ADD SALT

Cover the bowl with a damp cloth and let the dough rest for 30 minutes. After the dough has rested, leave the dough in the bowl and sprinkle half the salt over the dough, then flip it over and sprinkle the rest of the salt over the other side. Leaving the dough in the bowl, gently knead the salt into the dough until it is fully incorporated.

KNEAD

Turn the dough out onto a lightly floured work surface and knead until the gluten is fully developed. As you knead, you may need to dust your work surface with flour occasionally to stop the dough from sticking. If the dough tightens up so that it is not easily kneaded without shredding the surface of the dough, cover it with the mixing bowl and let it rest for 3 to 5 minutes, during which time the dough will relax and become workable again. Continue kneading until the dough is supple and smooth.

FIRST RISE

Place the dough back in the bowl and cover the bowl with a damp cloth. Let the dough rise for a half hour. Again remove it from the bowl and gently stretch and fold the dough. Place the dough back in the bowl and let rest for another half hour, then perform another stretch and fold. Place the dough back in the bowl, cover, and let rise until fully proofed. Use the poke test to ascertain when to shape the dough.

PORTION AND SHAPE

Remove the dough from the bowl and divide into two equal pieces, each weighing 1 pound, 8 ounces. Shape each piece into a round. Place the shaped breads seam down on a sheet pan that has been dusted with cornmeal or semolina, or seam up in proofing baskets that have been dusted with flour.

SECOND RISE AND SCORE

Cover the breads with a damp cloth and let rise in a draft-free area. Employ the poke test to judge when to bake the breads.

Just before the breads are to be loaded into the oven, score using a bread lamé. Hold the razor at a 90-degree angle and cut four equal slashes to form a square on top of each loaf. Overlap the ends of the cuts by 1½ inches.

BAKE

The breads may be baked on a baking stone or on a sheet pan. If using a baking stone, 1 hour prior to baking, place your stone on the center oven shelf and, using the non-convection mode, preheat the oven to 500°F. If baking on a sheet pan, preheat the oven 20 minutes prior to the bake. Ten minutes before baking, place a sheet pan (one with sides) on the bottom shelf of the oven and fill with 1½ cups boiling water. Just prior to baking the breads, add more boiling water to the sheet pan. If using a baking stone, transfer the breads seam down to a peel that has been lightly dusted with semolina or cornmeal and immediately peel the breads onto the baking stone. If using a sheet pan, place the pan with the breads on it directly into the oven on the middle shelf.

Bake for 30 to 35 minutes. Most home ovens bake unevenly, so you may need to turn the breads after 20 minutes. When fully baked, remove the breads from the oven and place on a cooling rack.

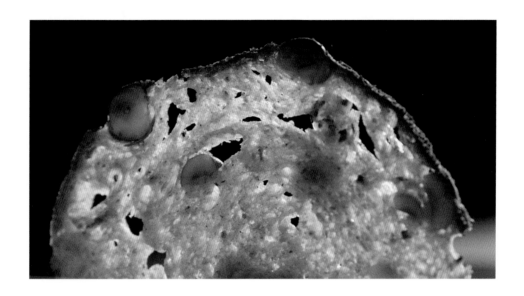

Rosemary Hazelnut Bread

YIELDS 2 LOAVES

Bakers often pair nuts and fruits together in breads, but tend to favor breads on the sweet side when using these ingredients. I am a fan of savory breads, such as this one that pairs the resinous flavor of rosemary with the toasted buttery flavor of hazelnuts. While no hazelnuts are grown commercially in Maine, the American hazelnut (Corylus americana) is native to the state. In Aroostook County, folks will go foraging for them in the fall. This bread gives you all the reason you will ever need to include rosemary in your home garden.

Recipe

Sourdough Starter

	GRAMS	OUNCES	VOLUME
FLOUR	140	4.9	¾ CUP + 3 TBSP
WATER	84	3.0	⅓ CUP + 1 TBSP
WHOLE WHEAT SOURDOUGH MOTHER	35	1.2	⅛ CUP + 1 TBSP
TOTAL	259	9.1	

Prep

	GRAMS	OUNCES	VOLUME
HAZELNUTS	182	6.4	1⅓ CUPS
FRESH ROSEMARY (DE-STEMMED)	17	0.6	¾ CUP

Dough	GRAMS	OUNCES	VOLUME
SIFTED WHOLE WHEAT FLOUR	261	9.2	1⅔ CUPS + 1 TBSP
BREAD FLOUR	261	9.2	1⅔ CUPS + 1 TBSP
WHOLE WHEAT SOURDOUGH STARTER	209	7.4	1 CUP + 1 TBSP
WATER	417	14.7	1¾ CUPS + 3 TBSP
ROSEMARY	17	0.6	¾ CUP
HAZELNUTS	182	6.4	1⅓ CUPS
SALT	13	0.5	1 TBSP
TOTAL	1,360	48	

Procedure

MIX THE SOURDOUGH STARTER

Measure the ingredients for the sourdough starter into a bowl and mix until they come together to form a uniform ball of dough. The dough temperature when mixed should be between 72°F and 80°F. Let rest for 6 to 8 hours. When fully fermented the starter will show some cracks on the surface, will have softened up, and will barely spring back when poked.

PREP

Fresh rosemary is sold on the stem; the leaves need to be removed from the stem before use. Coarsely chop the rosemary leaves.

Spread the hazelnuts in a single layer on a baking sheet and toast at 275°F for 15 to 20 minutes. To remove the skins, wrap the warm hazelnuts in a dish towel and let them sit for 5 to 10 minutes, then rub vigorously in the towel. You may use whole hazelnuts in this recipe or chop them up coarsely.

MEASURE AND MIX THE DOUGH

Measure out the salt and set aside both the salt and the hazelnuts. Measure into a large bowl the flours, sourdough starter, water, and rosemary. Using a spatula or plastic scraper, mix the ingredients together until evenly incorporated into a ball of dough. The dough temperature should be between 70°F and 80°F. Make sure to save the leftover sourdough starter to use as a sourdough mother in later bakes!

REST AND ADD SALT

Cover the bowl with a damp cloth and let the dough rest for 30 minutes. After the dough has rested, leave the dough in the bowl and sprinkle half the salt over the dough, then flip it over and sprinkle the rest of the salt over the other side. Leaving the dough in the bowl, gently knead the salt into the dough until it is fully incorporated.

KNEAD AND ADD HAZELNUTS

Turn the dough out onto a lightly floured work surface and knead until the gluten is fully developed. As you knead, you may need to dust your work surface with flour occasionally to stop the dough from sticking. If the dough tightens up so that it is not easily kneaded without shredding the surface of the dough, cover it with the mixing bowl and let it rest for 3 to 5 minutes, during which time the dough will relax and become workable again. Continue kneading until the dough is supple and smooth.

Cover the dough with the mixing bowl and let it rest for 5 minutes. Flatten the dough out and press the hazelnuts into both sides of the dough, then fold the dough up and knead it a couple of turns to evenly distribute the hazelnuts.

FIRST RISE

Place the dough back in the bowl and cover the bowl with a damp cloth. Let the dough rise until fully proofed. Use the poke test to ascertain when to shape the dough.

PORTION AND SHAPE

Remove the dough from the bowl and divide into two equal pieces, each weighing 1 pound, 8 ounces. Loosely pre-shape the pieces into rounds. Cover with a damp cloth and let rest for 5 minutes. Shape each piece into a 14-inch-long torpedo with tapered ends. Place the shaped breads seam down on a sheet pan that has been dusted with cornmeal or semolina, or seam up on a linen bread couche that has been dusted with flour (leave a fold of the linen between the two breads to separate them).

SECOND RISE AND SCORE

Cover the breads with a damp cloth and let rise in a draft-free area. Employ the poke test to judge when to bake the breads. If the breads are proofing on a linen bread couche, they will need to be transferred seam down to another sheet pan that has been dusted with semolina or cornmeal. If proofed on a sheet pan, they may stay on that pan and be loaded directly into the oven.

Just before the breads are to be loaded into the oven, score using a bread lamé. Hold the razor at a 45-degree angle and, starting 1 inch from the end of the loaf, with a single quick slash score the length of the bread to 1 inch from the other end.

BAKE

The breads may be baked on a baking stone or on a sheet pan. If baking on a baking stone, 1 hour prior to baking, place your stone on the center oven shelf and, using the non-convection mode, preheat the oven to 500°F. If baking on a sheet pan, preheat the oven 20 minutes prior to the bake. Ten minutes prior to baking, place a sheet pan (one with sides) on the bottom shelf of the oven and fill with 1½ cups boiling water. Just prior to baking the breads, add more boiling water to the sheet pan. If using a baking stone, transfer the breads seam down to a peel that has been lightly dusted with semolina or cornmeal and immediately peel the breads onto the baking stone. If using a sheet pan, place the pan with the breads on it directly into the oven on the middle shelf.

Bake for 30 to 35 minutes. Most home ovens bake unevenly, so you may need to turn the breads after 20 minutes. When fully baked, remove the breads from the oven and place on a cooling rack.

THE MANY MAINE GRAIN BREAD

YIELDS 2 LOAVES

The bread formula below takes simple ingredients and transforms them to celebrate the revival of Maine-grown grains over the past twenty years. Home bakers in Maine can now find locally grown and milled whole wheat flour, sifted wheat flour, whole rye flour, whole spelt flour, flint cornmeal, rolled oats, and buckwheat flour in local food co-ops, farmers' markets, and grocery stores. Since all whole flours and meals are most flavorful when freshly milled, the small-batch milling and short distances from Maine's mills to bakers and consumers ensure that our local flours and meals are indeed wonderfully fresh with superb baking characteristics.

Recipe

Poolish

	GRAMS	OUNCES	VOLUME
WHITE BREAD FLOUR	123	4.4	1 CUP
WATER	123	4.4	½ CUP + 1 TBSP
YEAST	3	0.1	1 TSP
TOTAL	249	8.9	

Prep Oat Mash

	GRAMS	OUNCES	VOLUME
ROLLED OATS	30	1.1	⅓ CUP
BOILING WATER	75	2.6	⅓ CUP
TOTAL	105	3.7	

Prep Corn Mash

	GRAMS	OUNCES	VOLUME
CORNMEAL	25	0.9	⅓ CUP
WATER	100	3.5	½ CUP
TOTAL	125	4.4	

Dough

	GRAMS	OUNCES	VOLUME
WHOLE WHEAT FLOUR	384	13.5	3 CUPS + 2 TBSP
WHITE BREAD FLOUR	115	4.1	1 CUP
WHOLE RYE FLOUR	50	1.8	½ CUP
POOLISH	249	8.8	1¼ CUPS
WATER	245	8.6	1¼ CUPS
CORN MASH	100	3.5	½ CUP
TOASTED OAT MASH	100	3.5	½ CUP
SALT	12	0.4	1 TBSP
TOTAL	1,255	44.2	

Procedure

As usual, I have presented the bread formula by weight in both grams and ounces and by volume in cups, tablespoons, and teaspoons. If you have a kitchen scale, I highly recommend you scale out the ingredients by weight, as this is far easier and more accurate than measuring by volume. This formula will yield two loaves weighing just over 1¼ pounds.

MIX THE POOLISH

For those wondering, "poolish" was named by the French for the Polish bakers who developed this type of pre-ferment in the early 1800s.

Combine the flour, water, and yeast in a bowl. Using a large spoon or spatula, mix until the poolish is uniformly smooth and not lumpy. The poolish temperature when mixed should be between 70°F and 75°F. Cover with a damp cloth and let the poolish develop for 10 to 12 hours. When fully developed, it will be quite bubbly, with new bubbles continuing to emerge and creases between sets of bubbles. I usually mix the poolish in the evening and use it sometime the next day.

PREP

Preheat the oven to 350°F. Evenly distribute the oats on a sheet pan and toast them in the oven for 7 minutes. Place the toasted oats in a bowl and pour the boiling water over them. Stir and let sit, but do not add to the dough until oats have cooled to room temperature.

Place the cornmeal and water in a heavy-bottomed saucepan. Cook for 30 minutes at a very low heat, stirring every 5 minutes to ensure it does not stick to the bottom of the pan. It should be thick and gloppy when done. Remove the corn mash from the pan and spread on a cookie sheet to cool to room temperature.

MEASURE AND MIX THE DOUGH

Measure out the water and poolish into a large bowl. Stir until the poolish is fully dispersed into the water, then add the flours and mashes. Reserve the salt for use later. As with the poolish, adjust the water temperature to ensure that the final dough temperature is between 70°F and 80°F. When it comes to mixing the dough, there are no better implements than your own two hands. So forego the wooden spoons, the spatulas, and the plastic scrapers and really get a "feel for the dough" by digging in with your digits. The mixing will go faster and you will get a much better sense of dough hydration and gluten development. Mix until all the flour is incorporated into a shaggy dough ball.

REST AND ADD SALT

Cover the bowl with a damp cloth and let the dough rest in a cool spot for 30 to 60 minutes. After the allotted time, sprinkle the salt over the dough and knead it in until fully incorporated.

KNEAD

Turn the dough out onto a work surface that has been lightly dusted with flour. Gently knead it until the dough has developed a silky-smooth, elastic feel.

FIRST RISE

Place the dough in a clean bowl and cover with a damp cloth. This first rise will take 2 to 3 hours depending on the ambient temperature. During this time the dough should almost double in size.

PORTION AND SHAPE

Remove the dough from the bowl and divide into two somewhat square equal pieces. To shape these rounds, we'll call the down side the face-side and the up side the seam-side. Take one piece of dough and fold it in half, then turn it 90 degrees and fold it in half again. Now orient the dough so the face-side is facing your belly button and the seam-side is facing away from you. While rolling the dough parallel to your body, stretch the face-side toward the seam-side and tuck the stretched dough into the center of the seam-side. This will create the needed tension in the ball of dough. Once you have rolled the dough approximately 2 feet, pick the dough up and bring it back to the starting spot. It doesn't matter which direction you work in. After two passes you should have a nice tight ball. Now pinch the seam shut.

Line a 1-quart bowl with a cotton tea towel, dish towel, or piece of linen. Dust the inside of the bowl with flour so that the cloth is uniformly covered with a thin layer. Place the bread seam up in the bowl and cover with a larger bowl or damp cloth.

SECOND RISE

Let the bread rise until it has almost doubled in size. Employ the poke test to judge when to bake the breads. Transfer breads from the cloth-lined bowls to a sheet pan that has been dusted with semolina or cornmeal by inverting the bowl onto the pan. Remove the bowl and cloth, and the bread should now be resting on the sheet pan seam down with the floured surface of the bread facing up.

SCORING, STEAMING, AND BAKING

Place a sheet pan on the bottom rack of the oven. Preheat the oven to 450°F. Put 2 cups water on the stovetop to boil.

Just before the breads are to be loaded into the oven, score using a bread lamé. Hold the razor with the blade parallel to the counter and score a 1-inch-deep circle three-quarters of the way up the loaf, then score eight equidistant vertical cuts ¾ inch deep and 1½ inches long, centered between the circular score at the top of the loaf and the bottom of the loaf.

Carefully pour the boiling water onto the sheet pan on the bottom shelf of the oven. Immediately put both loaves in the oven and bake for 35 to 40 minutes. After the first 10 minutes, the pan of water should be carefully removed from the oven to allow the bottom of the bread to bake fully. The steam in the oven gelatinizes the starches on the surface of the bread to create a chewy, crispy crust. When the bread is done, the scores should be dark brown with a slightly reddish cast. After the bread is out of the oven, you can check the internal temperature with a digital thermometer; a well-baked loaf should reach between 200°F and 210°F.

Savor the aroma of bread freshly liberated from the oven, but let the loaves cool to room temperature before noshing on them. This will ensure a nice moist crumb and maximum flavor. Then enjoy these loaves that evoke the true flavors of Maine.

Aroostook Wheat Bread

YIELDS 2 LOAVES

When we first started working with Maine-grown wheat in 1996, there were a host of issues—from wheat variety selection and fertilizer application to on-farm grain storage—that impacted the quality of wheat being grown. Flour quality in those first few years was quite variable. I knew there was a market for Maine-grown wheat, but that we would have to show some flexibility in the bakery. This was all part of the steep learning curve that Maine's farmers, millers, and bakers needed to undertake to reestablish wheat as a viable crop in Maine again. It was then that I developed the Aroostook Wheat Bread formula, blending 58 percent local whole wheat flour with 42 percent higher-gluten white bread flour from out West. Today, twenty years later, I am happy to say that the flour quality issues of those early years are no longer prevalent.

Recipe

Sourdough Starter	GRAMS	OUNCES	VOLUME
WHOLE WHEAT FLOUR	133	4.7	¾ CUP + 3 TBSP
WATER	80	2.8	⅓ CUP + 1 TBSP
WHOLE WHEAT SOURDOUGH MOTHER	40	1.4	¼ CUP
TOTAL	253	8.9	

Dough	GRAMS	OUNCES	VOLUME
BREAD FLOUR	333	11.7	2⅓ CUPS
WHOLE WHEAT FLOUR	333	11.7	2⅓ CUPS
SOURDOUGH STARTER	200	7.0	1 CUP
WATER	479	16.9	2 CUPS + 2 TSP
SALT	16	0.6	1 TBSP
TOTAL	1,361	47.9	

Procedure

MIX THE SOURDOUGH STARTER

Measure the ingredients for the sourdough starter into a bowl, and with a spatula or whisk mix vigorously until the ingredients have been uniformly mixed together with no lumps remaining. The sourdough temperature when mixed should be between 75°F and 80°F. Let this mixture ferment until fully developed, approximately 10 to 12 hours.

MEASURE AND MIX THE DOUGH

Measure out the salt and set aside. Measure into a large bowl the bread flour, whole wheat flour, sourdough starter, and water. Using a spatula or plastic scraper, mix the ingredients together until the flour is evenly incorporated into a ball of dough. The dough temperature should be between 70°F and 80°F. Make sure to save the leftover sourdough starter to use as a sourdough mother in later bakes!

REST AND ADD SALT

Cover the bowl with a damp cloth and let the dough rest for 30 minutes. After the dough has rested, leave the dough in the bowl and sprinkle half the salt over the dough, then flip it over and sprinkle the rest of the salt over the other side. Leaving the dough in the bowl, gently knead the salt into the dough until it is fully incorporated.

KNEAD

Turn the dough out onto a lightly floured work surface and knead until the gluten is well developed. As you knead, you may need to lightly dust your work surface with flour occasionally to stop the dough from sticking. If the dough tightens up so that it is not easily kneaded without shredding the surface of the dough, cover it with the mixing bowl and let it rest for 5 minutes, during which time the dough will relax and become workable again. Continue kneading until the dough is supple and smooth.

FIRST RISE

Place the dough back in the bowl and cover the bowl with a damp cloth. Let the dough rise for 45 minutes. Again remove it from the bowl, gently stretch and fold the dough, then place back in the bowl. Continue to let the dough rise until fully proofed, using the poke test to ascertain when to shape the dough.

PORTION AND SHAPE

Remove the dough from the bowl and divide into two equal pieces, each weighing 1 pound, 8 ounces. Shape each piece into a 10-inch-long cylinder with slightly tapered ends. Place the shaped breads seam down on a sheet pan that has been dusted with cornmeal or semolina, or seam up on a linen bread couche that has been dusted with flour (leave a fold of the linen between the two breads to separate them).

SECOND RISE AND SCORE

Cover the breads with a damp cloth and let rise in a draft-free area. Employ the poke test to judge when to bake the breads.

Just before the breads are to be loaded into the oven, whether on a sheet pan or being peeled onto a baking stone, score using a bread lamé. Hold the razor at a 45-degree angle and give each bread two diagonal slashes on the top.

BAKE

The breads may be baked on a baking stone or on a sheet pan. If baking on a baking stone, 1 hour prior to baking, place your stone on the center oven shelf and, using the non-convection mode, preheat the oven to 500°F. If baking on a sheet pan, preheat the oven 20 minutes prior to the bake. Ten minutes prior to baking, place a sheet pan (one with sides) on the bottom shelf of the oven and fill with 1½ cups boiling water. Just prior to baking the breads, add more boiling water to the sheet pan. If using a baking stone, transfer the breads seam down to a peel that has been lightly dusted with semolina or cornmeal and immediately peel the breads onto the baking stone. If using a sheet pan, place the pan with the breads on it directly into the oven on the middle shelf.

Bake for 30 to 35 minutes. Most home ovens bake unevenly, so you may need to turn the breads after 20 minutes. When fully baked, remove the breads from the oven and place on a cooling rack.

KATAHDIN BREAD

YIELDS 2 LOAVES

Named after Maine's highest peak, Mount Katahdin, this bread is a two-pound mountain of 100 percent whole grain goodness. It is a rugged, substantial loaf—crusty, chewy, dense, and utterly delicious—especially when made with freshly milled whole wheat flour.

Recipe

Sourdough Starter	GRAMS	OUNCES	VOLUME
WHOLE WHEAT FLOUR	169	6.0	¾ CUP + 1 TBSP
WATER	110	3.9	⅓ CUP + 1 TBSP
WHOLE WHEAT SOURDOUGH MOTHER	42	1.5	⅛ CUP + 1 TBSP
TOTAL	321	11.4	

Dough	GRAMS	OUNCES	VOLUME
WHOLE WHEAT FLOUR	892	31.5	4½ CUPS
SOURDOUGH STARTER	268	9.4	1 CUP
WATER	633	22.3	4⅛ CUPS + 1 TBSP
SALT	21	0.7	1 TBSP
TOTAL	1,814	63.9	

Procedure

MIX THE SOURDOUGH STARTER

Measure the ingredients for the sourdough starter into a bowl and with a spatula or whisk mix vigorously until the ingredients have been uniformly combined with no lumps remaining. The sourdough temperature when mixed should be between 75°F and 80°F. Let this mixture ferment until fully developed, approximately 10 to 12 hours.

MEASURE AND MIX THE DOUGH

Measure out the salt and set aside. Measure into a large bowl the whole wheat flour, sourdough starter, and water. Using a spatula or plastic scraper, mix the ingredients together until the flour is evenly incorporated into a ball of dough. The dough temperature should be between 70°F and 80°F. Make sure to save the leftover sourdough starter to use as a sourdough mother in later bakes!

REST AND ADD SALT

Cover the bowl with a damp cloth and let the dough rest for 30 minutes. After the dough has rested, leave the dough in the bowl and sprinkle half the salt over the dough, then flip it over and sprinkle the rest of the salt over the other side. Leaving the dough in the bowl, gently knead the salt into the dough until it is fully incorporated.

KNEAD

Turn the dough out onto a lightly floured work surface and knead until the gluten is well developed. As you knead, you may need to lightly dust your work surface with flour occasionally to stop the dough from sticking. If the dough tightens up so that it is not easily kneaded without shredding the surface of the dough, cover it with the mixing bowl and let it rest for 5 minutes, during which time the dough will relax and become workable again. Continue kneading until the dough is supple and smooth.

FIRST RISE

Place the dough back in the bowl and cover the bowl with a damp cloth. Let the dough rise for 45 minutes. Again remove it from the bowl, gently stretch and fold the dough, then place back in the bowl. Continue to let the dough rise until fully proofed, using the poke test to ascertain when to shape the dough.

PORTION AND SHAPE

Remove the dough from the bowl and divide into two equal pieces, each weighing 2 pounds. Shape each piece into a tight round, but do not seal the bottoms of the rounds. Dust them with flour and place the shaped breads seam down on a sheet pan that has been dusted with cornmeal or semolina, or seam down in proofing baskets that have been lightly dusted with flour.

SECOND RISE AND SCORE

Cover the breads with a damp cloth and let rise in a draft-free area. Employ the poke test to judge when to bake the breads.

Just before the breads are to be loaded into the oven, flip them over and gently pull apart the seam. As the breads rise in the oven, the seam will open up and allow the bread to fully expand, just as scoring the loaves would do.

BAKE

The breads may be baked on a baking stone or on a sheet pan. If baking on a baking stone, 1 hour prior to baking, place your stone on the center oven shelf and, using the non-convection mode, preheat the oven to 500°F. If baking on a sheet pan, preheat the oven 20 minutes prior to the bake. Ten minutes prior to baking, place a sheet pan (one with sides) on the bottom shelf of the oven and fill with 1½ cups boiling water. Just prior to baking the breads, add more boiling water to the sheet pan. If using a baking stone, transfer the breads seam down to a peel that has been lightly dusted with semolina or cornmeal and immediately peel the breads onto the baking stone. If using a sheet pan, place the pan with the breads on it directly into the oven on the middle shelf.

Bake for 30 to 35 minutes. Most home ovens bake unevenly, so you may need to turn the breads after 20 minutes. When fully baked, remove the breads from the oven and place on a cooling rack.

SAVORY WALNUT BREAD

YIELDS 2 LOAVES

If you have never baked a walnut sourdough bread before, then you are in for quite a surprise. In the acidic environment of the bread dough, the gallic acid in the walnut skins reacts with iron present in the flour to produce a purple-colored dough. If you want to surprise folks with a purple bread, chop up the walnuts finer and add them at the beginning of the mixing procedure rather than folding them in at the end. Lightly toasting the walnuts adds a wonderful earthiness to the bread that complements the zing of the black pepper.

Recipe

Sourdough Starter

	GRAMS	OUNCES	VOLUME
BREAD FLOUR	109	3.8	¾ CUP + 2 TBSP
WATER	109	3.8	½ CUP + 1 TBSP
WHITE SOURDOUGH MOTHER	36	1.3	⅛ CUP + 1 TBSP
TOTAL	254	8.9	

Prep	GRAMS	OUNCES	VOLUME
WALNUTS	139	4.9	1⅓ CUPS

Dough	GRAMS	OUNCES	VOLUME
SIFTED WHEAT FLOUR (86%)	574	20.2	
SOURDOUGH STARTER	201	7.1	¾ CUP + 2 TBSP
WATER	430	15.2	2 CUPS
BLACK PEPPER	3	0.1	1 TBSP
SALT	13	0.5	1 TBSP
WALNUTS	139	4.9	1⅓ CUPS
TOTAL	1,360	48	

Procedure

MIX THE SOURDOUGH STARTER

Measure the ingredients for the sourdough starter into a bowl, and with a spatula or whisk mix vigorously until the ingredients have been uniformly mixed together with no lumps remaining. The sourdough temperature when mixed should be between 75°F and 80°F. Let this mixture ferment until fully developed, approximately 10 to 12 hours.

PREP

Preheat the oven to 300°F. Weigh out the walnuts, then place them on a sheet pan and toast in the oven for 8 to 9 minutes. Care needs to be taken when toasting walnuts, however; toast them too long and they become unpleasantly bitter. Remove walnuts from the oven, let cool, and chop into halves.

MEASURE AND MIX THE DOUGH

Measure out the salt and set aside. Measure into a large bowl the sifted wheat flour, sourdough starter, water, and black pepper. Using a spatula or plastic scraper, mix the ingredients together until evenly incorporated into a ball of dough. The dough temperature should be between 70°F and 80°F. Make sure to save the leftover sourdough starter to use as a sourdough mother in later bakes!

REST AND ADD SALT

Cover the bowl with a damp cloth and let the dough rest for 30 minutes. After the dough has rested, leave the dough in the bowl and sprinkle half the salt over the dough, then flip it over and sprinkle the rest of the salt over the other side. Leaving the dough in the bowl, gently knead the salt into the dough until it is fully incorporated.

KNEAD AND ADD WALNUTS

Turn the dough out onto a lightly floured work surface and knead until the gluten is fully developed. As you knead, you may need to dust your work surface with flour occasionally to stop the dough from sticking. If the dough tightens up so that it is not easily kneaded without shredding the surface of the dough, cover it with the mixing bowl and let it rest for 3 to 5 minutes, during which time the dough will relax and become workable again. Continue kneading until the dough is supple and smooth.

Cover the dough with the mixing bowl and let it rest for 5 minutes. Flatten the dough out and press the walnuts into both sides of the dough, then fold the dough up and knead it a couple of turns to evenly distribute the walnuts.

FIRST RISE

Place the dough back in the bowl and cover the bowl with a damp cloth. Let the dough rise for a half hour. Again remove it from the bowl and gently stretch and fold the dough. Place the dough back in the bowl and let rest for another half hour, then perform another stretch and fold. Place the dough back in the bowl, cover, and let rise until fully proofed. Use the poke test to ascertain when to shape the dough.

PORTION AND SHAPE

Remove the dough from the bowl and divide into two equal pieces, each weighing about 1 pound, 8 ounces. Pre-shape each piece of dough into a round. Cover and let rest for 15 minutes. Shape each round into a long torpedo loaf with the dough tapering evenly into a point at either end. Place the shaped breads seam down on a sheet pan that has been dusted with cornmeal or semolina, or on a linen bread couche that has been dusted with bread or rice flour (leave a fold of the linen between the two breads to separate them).

SECOND RISE AND SCORE

Cover the breads with a damp cloth and let rise in a draft-free area. Employ the poke test to judge when to bake the breads. If the breads are proofing in a linen bread couche, they will need to be transferred seam down to another sheet pan that has been dusted with semolina or cornmeal. If proofed on a sheet pan, they may stay on that pan and be loaded directly into the oven.

Just before the breads are to be loaded into the oven, score using a bread lamé. Hold the razor at a 45-degree angle and give each bread three evenly spaced diagonal scores on the top.

BAKE

The breads may be baked on a baking stone or on a sheet pan. If baking on a stone, 1 hour prior to baking, place your stone on the center oven shelf and, using the non-convection mode, preheat the oven to 500°F. If baking on a sheet pan, preheat the oven 20 minutes prior to the bake. Ten minutes prior to baking, place a sheet pan (one with sides) on the bottom shelf of the oven and fill with 1½ cups boiling water. Just prior to baking the breads, add more boiling water to the sheet pan. If using a baking stone, transfer the breads seam down to a peel that has been lightly dusted with semolina or cornmeal and immediately peel the breads onto the baking stone. If using a sheet pan, place the pan with the breads on it directly into the oven on the middle shelf.

Bake for 30 to 35 minutes. Most home ovens bake unevenly, so you may need to turn the breads after 20 minutes. When fully baked, remove the breads from the oven and place on a cooling rack.

PUMPKIN RAISIN BREAD

YIELDS 2 LOAVES

This is one of the seasonal breads we make at the bakery. We usually start baking this bread at the end of October and stop making it at the end of February. Fresh baking pumpkins are usually available in the fall. During the rest of the year, butternut squash can be substituted for the pumpkin. While you can for convenience use canned pumpkin in this recipe, the flavor of the bread is greatly enhanced when made with freshly cooked pumpkin or squash. The bread has a touch of sweetness from the small amount of honey and the raisins, but is not nearly as sweet as pumpkin quick breads are. This pumpkin bread is the perfect choice if you want to make fabulous French toast with a twist. If I am making rolls for Thanksgiving, I'll use this recipe but without the raisins.

Recipe

Sourdough Starter

	GRAMS	OUNCES	VOLUME
FLOUR	97	3.4	⅔ CUP
WATER	97	3.4	⅓ CUP + 2 TBSP
WHITE SOURDOUGH MOTHER	24	0.9	⅛ CUP
TOTAL	218	7.7	

Prep

	GRAMS	OUNCES	VOLUME
RAISINS	112	4.0	¾ CUP
WATER	220	7.8	1 CUP

BAKE 1 PUMPKIN/BUTTERNUT SQUASH	(CUT IN HALF AND BAKE AT 350°F FOR 45–60 MINUTES)

Dough

	GRAMS	OUNCES	VOLUME
BREAD FLOUR	561	19.8	3¾ CUPS
WHITE SOURDOUGH STARTER	168	5.9	¾ CUP
WATER	308	10.9	1⅓ CUPS + 2 TBSP
PUMPKIN/SQUASH	168	5.9	⅔ CUP
HONEY	28	1.0	1 TBSP
CINNAMON	1	0.02	½ TSP
CLOVES	0.4	0.01	¼ TSP
NUTMEG	0.4	0.01	¼ TSP
SALT	13	0.45	1 TBSP
RAISINS	112	4.0	¾ CUP
TOTAL	1,360	48	

Procedure

MIX THE SOURDOUGH STARTER

Measure the ingredients for the sourdough starter into a bowl, and with a spatula or whisk mix vigorously until the ingredients have been uniformly mixed together with no lumps remaining. The sourdough temperature when mixed should be between 75°F and 80°F. Let this mixture ferment until fully developed, approximately 10 to 12 hours.

PREP

Raisins: A few hours before you mix the dough, measure out the raisins and let them soak in a cup of room temperature water. Plumping up the raisins in water ensures that they do not pull moisture from the dough. Reserve the water the raisins were soaked in for use as part of the total water to be added to the bread dough.

Pumpkin/squash: Preheat the oven to 350°F. Cut the pumpkin in half and scoop out the seeds. Put a cup of water in a roasting pan and place the two halves cut side down in the pan. Bake for 45 to 60 minutes until soft. Remove from the oven and let cool. Scoop out the flesh and puree in a blender or food processor.

MEASURE AND MIX THE DOUGH

Measure out the salt and set aside. Measure into a large bowl the bread flour, sourdough starter, water, pumpkin/squash, honey, and spices. Using a spatula or plastic scraper, mix the ingredients together until evenly incorporated into a ball of dough. The dough temperature should be between 70°F and 80°F. Make sure to save the leftover sourdough starter to use as a sourdough mother in later bakes!

REST AND ADD SALT

Cover the bowl with a damp cloth and let the dough rest for 30 minutes. After the dough has rested, leave the dough in the bowl and sprinkle half the salt over the dough, then flip it over and sprinkle the rest of the salt over the other side. Leaving the dough in the bowl, gently knead the salt into the dough until it is fully incorporated.

KNEAD AND ADD RAISINS

Turn the dough out onto a lightly floured work surface and knead until the gluten is fully developed. As you knead, you may need to dust your work surface with flour occasionally to stop the dough from sticking. If the dough tightens up so that it is not easily kneaded without shredding the surface of the dough, cover it with the mixing bowl and let it rest for 3 to 5 minutes. During that time the dough will relax and become workable again. Continue kneading until the dough is supple and smooth.

Cover the dough with the mixing bowl and let it rest for 5 minutes. Flatten the dough out and press the raisins into both sides of the dough, then fold the dough up and knead it a couple of turns to evenly distribute the raisins.

FIRST RISE

Place the dough back in the bowl and cover the bowl with a damp cloth. Let the dough rise until fully proofed. Use the poke test to ascertain when to shape the dough.

PORTION AND SHAPE

Remove the dough from the bowl and divide into two equal pieces, each weighing 1 pound, 8 ounces. Shape each piece of dough into a round. Place the breads seam down on a sheet pan that has been dusted with semolina or cornmeal, or seam down in proofing baskets that have been lightly dusted with flour.

SECOND RISE AND SCORE

Cover the breads with a damp cloth and let rise in a draft-free area. Employ the poke test to judge when to bake the breads. If the breads are in proofing baskets, they will need to be transferred seam down to a sheet pan that has been dusted with semolina or cornmeal, or placed on a peel that has also been dusted, if they are to bake on a baking stone. If proofed on a sheet pan, they may stay on that pan and be loaded directly into the oven.

Just before the breads are to be loaded into the oven, score using a bread lamé. Hold the razor at a 45-degree angle and slash a 3-inch-diameter circle on the top of each loaf.

BAKE

The breads may be baked on a baking stone or on a sheet pan. If baking on a stone, 1 hour prior to baking, place your stone on the center oven shelf and, using the non-convection mode, preheat the oven to 500°F. If baking on a sheet pan, preheat the oven 20 minutes prior to the bake. Ten minutes prior to baking, place a sheet pan (one with sides) on the bottom shelf of the oven and fill with 1½ cups boiling water. Just prior to baking the breads, add more boiling water to the sheet pan. If using a baking stone, transfer the breads seam down to a peel that has been lightly dusted with semolina or cornmeal and immediately peel the breads onto the baking stone. If using a sheet pan, place the pan with the breads on it directly into the oven on the middle shelf.

Bake for 30 to 35 minutes. Most home ovens bake unevenly, so you may need to turn the breads after 20 minutes. When fully baked, remove the breads from the oven and place on a cooling rack.

Old-Fashioned Anadama Bread

YIELDS 2 LOAVES

When I first started the bakery, I knew we would need to carve out a niche for our-selves based on the quality and character of our breads. Part of what has defined that niche is our hearth-baked breads, which come in a variety of shapes and sizes. We have never made pan breads at the bakery, in part because we do not want our breads to be considered in any way comparable to the loaves produced by large commercial bakeries that are found in the bread isles of supermarkets in all their rectangular glory. Some of our recipes, however, work well whether in a pan or not. For those bakers who are more comfortable making pan breads, or for those who prefer the consistent shape of bread slices from a pan, I provide this and the following recipe. Like most of our breads, both are leavened with sourdough starters and are still distinguished by that hearty tang and open crumb.

The ingredients for this bread have been staples in New England farm kitchens since colonial times. While there are many dubious stories about how anadama bread got its name, no one truly knows its provenance. Maize cultivation was adopted by European settlers from the local Native American peoples, and Indian flint corn was a common crop on Maine farms through the end of the eighteenth century. Molasses was imported from the Caribbean islands as part of the triangle trade routes between Europe, Africa, and the Americas and was a common ingredient in farm kitchens of the time. Recently Johanna Davis and Adam Nordell of Songbird Farm in Unity, Maine, have started growing and milling an Abenaki flint corn that harkens back to those times, and is perfect for making this bread.

In this recipe the sweetness imparted by the molasses nicely complements the tang of the sourdough fermentation. In many anadama bread recipes, the flavor of the molas-ses dominates to the detriment of the other ingredients. Here I have been careful not to oversweeten it, so the flavor of the cornmeal shines through. Any whole cornmeal will work in this recipe if you cannot find a flint cornmeal. However, the de-germed cornmeal often found in supermarkets is devoid of flavor and should be avoided. While this bread can be baked on a sheet pan or baking stone, it is traditionally baked in a loaf pan as in the recipe here.

Recipe

Sourdough Starter

	GRAMS	OUNCES	VOLUME
WHOLE WHEAT FLOUR	117	4.1	¾ CUP
WATER	76	2.7	⅓ CUP + 1 TSP
WHOLE WHEAT SOURDOUGH MOTHER	35	1.2	⅛ CUP + 1 TSP
TOTAL	228	8	

Prep Corn Mash

	GRAMS	OUNCES	VOLUME
FLINT CORNMEAL	49	1.7	⅓ CUP + 2 TSP
BUTTER	28	1.0	2 TBSP
WATER	194	6.8	¾ CUP + 3 TBSP
TOTAL	271	9.5	

Dough

	GRAMS	OUNCES	VOLUME
BREAD FLOUR	577	20.4	3¾ CUPS
SOURDOUGH STARTER	173	6.1	¾ CUP
WATER	260	9.2	1⅛ CUPS + 1 TBSP
MOLASSES	104	3.7	⅓ CUP
CORN MASH	231	8.1	¾ CUP + 4 TBSP
SALT	15	0.5	1 TBSP
TOTAL	1,360	48	

Procedure

MIX THE SOURDOUGH STARTER

Measure the ingredients for the sourdough starter into a bowl and combine until they come together to form a uniform ball of dough. The dough temperature when mixed should be between 72°F and 80°F. Let rest for 6 to 8 hours. When fully fermented the starter will show some cracks on the surface, have softened up, and barely spring back when poked.

PREP

The cornmeal used in this recipe needs to be cooked prior to adding it to the dough. Place the cornmeal, butter, and water in a heavy-bottomed saucepan and let simmer slowly at a very low temperature, stirring the cornmeal every 5 minutes to ensure that it does not stick to the bottom of the pan. When done, the corn mash should be soft and not gritty. It's a good idea to taste it to be sure the consistency is correct. Remove from the heat and let cool to room temperature before adding to the dough.

MEASURE AND MIX THE DOUGH

Measure out the salt and sourdough starter and set aside. Measure into a large bowl the flour, water, molasses, and the cooled corn mash. Using a spatula or plastic scraper, mix the ingredients together until evenly incorporated into a ball of dough. The dough temperature should be between 70°F and 80°F.

REST AND ADD SALT AND SOURDOUGH STARTER

Cover the bowl with a damp cloth and let the dough rest for 30 minutes. After the dough has rested, leave the dough in the bowl and knead the salt and sourdough starter into the dough until evenly incorporated. Make sure to save the leftover sourdough starter to use as a sourdough mother in later bakes!

KNEAD

Turn the dough out onto a lightly floured work surface and knead until the gluten is fully developed. As you knead, you may need to dust your work surface with flour occasionally to stop the dough from sticking. If the dough tightens up so that it is not easily kneaded without shredding the surface of the dough, cover it with the mixing bowl and let it rest for 3 to 5 minutes, during which time the dough will relax and become workable again. Continue kneading until the dough is supple and smooth.

FIRST RISE

Place the dough back in the bowl and cover the bowl with a damp cloth. Let the dough rise for 45 minutes. Again remove it from the bowl and gently stretch and fold the dough. Place the dough back in the bowl, cover, and let rise until fully proofed. Use the poke test to ascertain when to shape the dough.

PORTION AND SHAPE

Lightly grease two standard-size loaf pans (8 × 4 × 3 inches). Remove the dough from the bowl and divide into two equal pieces. Shape each piece into a cylinder long enough to almost fill the length of the loaf pan.

SECOND RISE

Cover the breads with a damp cloth and set in a draft-free area. Let the bread dough rise until it fills the pan, is nicely domed, and passes the poke test.

BAKE

Preheat the oven to 400°F. Place the loaf pans in the center of the middle rack in the oven. Be sure to leave clearance above for the loaves to rise.

Bake for 45 to 55 minutes. Halfway through the bake, rotate the bread pans 180 degrees. Bake until the loaves are well browned. The internal temperature of the breads should be 205°F when fully baked. Remove the loaves from the pans (they should sound hollow when tapped on the bottom). Allow to cool on a rack.

TOASTED OAT BREAD

YIELDS 2 LOAVES

I love a bowl of hot oatmeal on a wintry morning, and the oats grown at Aurora Mills and Farm way up in Aroostook County are incredibly nourishing and tasty. When I was developing the recipe for this bread, I wanted to capture the flavor of that oatmeal in the bread as well. To enhance the flavor of the oats, I toast them first and then create a mash, hydrating them with boiling water.

Recipe

Sourdough Starter	GRAMS	OUNCES	VOLUME
WHOLE WHEAT FLOUR	83	2.9	½ CUP + 1 TBSP
WATER	50	1.8	¼ CUP
WHOLE WHEAT SOURDOUGH MOTHER	25	0.9	⅛ CUP
TOTAL	158	5.6	

Prep Oat Mash	GRAMS	OUNCES	VOLUME
ROLLED OATS	94	3.3	¾ CUP + 1 TBSP
WATER, BOILING	189	6.7	¾ CUP + 2 TBSP
TOTAL	283	10	

Dough	GRAMS	OUNCES	VOLUME
SIFTED WHEAT FLOUR	420	14.8	2¾ CUPS + 1 TBSP
BREAD FLOUR	139	4.9	1 CUP
WHOLE WHEAT SOURDOUGH STARTER	168	5.9	¾ CUP
OAT MASH	260	9.2	AS PREPPED
WATER	359	12.7	1½ CUPS + 1 TBSP
SALT	13	0.5	1 TBSP
TOTAL	1,359	48	

MIX THE SOURDOUGH STARTER

Measure the ingredients for the sourdough starter into a bowl and combine until they come together to form a uniform ball of dough. The dough temperature when mixed should be between 72°F and 80°F. Let rest for 6 to 8 hours. When fully fermented the starter will show some cracks on the surface, will have softened up, and will barely spring back when poked.

PREP

Preheat the oven to 300°F. Measure out the oats and spread them evenly on a sheet pan. Bake for 8 to 10 minutes. Place the toasted oats in a bowl and pour the boiling water over them. Stir and let sit, but do not add to the dough until oats have cooled to room temperature.

MEASURE AND MIX THE DOUGH

Measure out the salt and sourdough starter and set aside. Measure into a large bowl the sifted wheat flour, bread flour, oat mash, and water. Using a spatula or plastic scraper, mix the ingredients together until evenly incorporated into a ball of dough. The dough temperature should be between 70°F and 80°F.

REST AND ADD SALT AND SOURDOUGH STARTER

Cover the bowl with a damp cloth and let the dough rest for 30 minutes. After the dough has rested, leave the dough in the bowl and knead the salt and sourdough starter into the dough until evenly incorporated. Make sure to save the leftover sourdough starter to use as a sourdough mother in later bakes!

KNEAD

Turn the dough out onto a lightly floured work surface and knead until the gluten is fully developed. As you knead, you may need to dust your work surface with flour occasionally to stop the dough from sticking. If the dough tightens up so that it is not easily kneaded without shredding the surface of the dough, cover it with the mixing bowl and let it rest for 3 to 5 minutes, during which time the dough will relax and become workable again. Continue kneading until the dough is supple and smooth.

FIRST RISE

Place the dough back in the bowl and cover the bowl with a damp cloth. Let the dough rise for 45 minutes. Again remove it from the bowl and gently stretch and fold the dough. Place the dough back in the bowl, cover, and let rise until fully proofed. Use the poke test to ascertain when to shape the dough.

PORTION AND SHAPE

Lightly grease two standard-size loaf pans (8 × 4 × 3 inches). Remove the dough from the bowl and divide into two equal pieces. Shape each piece into a cylinder long enough to almost fill the length of the loaf pan.

SECOND RISE

Cover the breads with a damp cloth and set in a draft-free area. Let the bread dough rise until it fills the pan, is nicely domed, and passes the poke test.

BAKE

Preheat the oven to 400°F. Place the loaf pans in the center of the middle rack in the oven. Be sure to leave clearance above for the loaves to rise.

Bake for 45 to 55 minutes. Halfway through the bake, rotate the bread pans 180 degrees. Bake until the loaves are well browned. The internal temperature of the breads should be 205°F when fully baked. Remove the loaves from the pans (they should sound hollow when tapped on the bottom). Allow to cool on a rack.

LEMON SAGE FOCACCIA

YIELDS 2 ROUND OR 1 RECTANGULAR FOCACCIA(S)

Flatbreads are the breads of immigrants. The Acadians brought ployes; Italians, focaccia and pizza; Lebanese, pita bread; and Somalis, anjero. Interestingly, one of Maine's oldest immigrant communities, the Acadians, share with our newest, the Somalis, a style of flatbread that is remarkably similar though uses a different blend of grains. At Borealis Breads focaccia has been our flatbread of choice. Every year at the Common Ground Fair, our rosemary focaccia has been one of our best-selling breads, and for many years we offered a three-cheese focaccia. My favorite flatbread is the Maine Coast Focaccia that we make for our summer farmers' markets.

We almost always have sage growing in our kitchen garden, and this is my favorite way to employ this herb. The secret to really bringing out the sage flavor in the bread is to bruise the leaves before chopping them up. Crush them into a small ball in the palm of your hand and roll it firmly between your palms until the leaves turn from a pale dusky green to a darker green. Bruising the leaves will release far more of the essential oils that impart flavor to the bread than chopping alone.

Recipe

Sourdough Starter	GRAMS	OUNCES	VOLUME
FLOUR	119	4.2	¾ CUP
WATER	119	4.2	½ CUP + 2 TSP
WHITE SOURDOUGH MOTHER	36	1.3	⅛ CUP
TOTAL	274	9.7	

Prep	GRAMS	OUNCES	VOLUME
LEMON-SAGE INFUSION			
LEMON ZEST	9	0.3	3 TBSP (3 LEMONS)
SAGE LEAVES	11	0.4	½ CUP
WATER, BOILING	148	5.2	⅔ CUP + 2 TSP
TOTAL	168	5.9	

Dough	GRAMS	OUNCES	VOLUME
BREAD FLOUR	632	22.3	4⅛ CUPS + 1 TBSP
WHITE SOURDOUGH STARTER	221	7.8	1 CUP
LEMON-SAGE INFUSION	168	5.9	AS PREPPED
WATER	274	9.7	1⅓ CUPS
SALT	15	0.5	1 TBSP
OLIVE OIL	51	1.8	¼ CUP
TOTAL	1,361	48	

Procedure

MIX THE SOURDOUGH STARTER

Measure the ingredients for the sourdough starter into a bowl, and with a spatula or whisk mix vigorously until the ingredients have been uniformly mixed together with no lumps remaining. The sourdough temperature when mixed should be between 72°F and 80°F. Let this mixture ferment until fully developed, approximately 10 to 12 hours.

PREP

Zest three lemons. Remove the sage leaves from the stems and bruise the leaves, then chop coarsely. Place the zest and sage in a small bowl and pour the boiling water over them. Let the mixture cool to room temperature before adding to the dough.

MEASURE AND MIX THE DOUGH

Measure out the salt and set aside. Measure into a large bowl the bread flour, sourdough starter, lemon-sage infusion, and water. Using a spatula or plastic scraper, mix the ingredients together until evenly incorporated into a ball of dough. The dough temperature should be between 70°F and 80°F. Make sure to save the leftover sourdough starter to use as a sourdough mother in later bakes!

REST AND ADD SALT

Cover the bowl with a damp cloth and let the dough rest for 30 minutes. After the dough has rested, leave the dough in the bowl and sprinkle half the salt over the dough, flip it over and sprinkle the rest of the salt over the other side. Leaving the dough in the bowl, gently knead the salt into the dough until it is fully incorporated.

KNEAD

Turn the dough out onto a lightly floured work surface and knead until the gluten is fully developed. As you knead, you may need to dust your work surface with flour occasionally to stop the dough from sticking. If the dough tightens up so that it is not easily kneaded without shredding the surface of the dough, cover it with the mixing bowl and let it rest for 3 to 5 minutes, during which time the dough will relax and become workable again. Continue kneading until the dough is supple and smooth.

FIRST RISE

Place the dough back in the bowl and cover the dough with a damp cloth. Let the dough rise for a half hour. Again remove it from the bowl and gently stretch and fold the dough. Place the dough back in the bowl, cover, and let rise until fully proofed. Use the poke test to ascertain when to shape the dough.

PORTION AND SHAPE

There is enough dough to fill a half sheet pan (12 × 17 inches) or to make two 24-ounce round focaccias. If making rounds, divide the dough into two equal pieces and pre-shape into two loosely formed rounds. Let dough rest for 10 minutes, then gently stretch each piece into a 10-inch-diameter circle. Place on sheet pans that have been dusted with cornmeal or semolina. If making a rectangular focaccia, place a piece of parchment paper on a sheet pan with the paper extending over the sides of the pan by 3 inches. On a lightly floured work surface, gently pull and stretch the dough into a rectangular shape that is of uniform thickness and slightly smaller than the sheet pan. Transfer dough to the parchment-lined pan.

SECOND RISE AND DIMPLING

Cover the dough loosely with a damp cloth and let rise in a draft-free area. Employ the poke test to judge when the breads are ready to bake. Just before the breads are to be loaded into the oven, use your fingers or the end of a spatula handle to dimple the focaccia with eight to ten evenly spaced dimples on each round, or sixteen to twenty evenly spaced dimples on the rectangular focaccia. If baking on a stone, dimple the dough when it is on the peel. If baking on the sheet pans the dough was rising on, dimple the dough in place. When dimpling the dough, unless it is over-proofed, press straight down to the bottom of the dough to create the dimples. Over-proofed dough will have larger pockets or bubbles that when baked leave holes in the bread. If you are baking bread for sandwiches, which we do at the bakery, the holes will not contain your sandwich fillings as well as a properly proofed bread. If you have left your dough too long and it is over-proofed, the best thing you can do is get it into the oven as quickly as possible.

BAKE

The focaccias may be baked on a baking stone or on a sheet pan. If using a baking stone, 1 hour prior to baking, place your stone on the center oven shelf and, using the non-convection mode, preheat the oven to 500°F. If baking on a sheet pan, preheat the oven 20 minutes prior to the bake. Ten minutes prior to baking, place a sheet pan (one with sides) on the bottom shelf of the oven and fill with 1½ cups boiling water. Just prior to baking the breads, add more boiling water to the sheet pan. If using a baking stone, transfer the focaccia to a peel that has been lightly dusted with semolina or cornmeal and immediately peel the breads onto the baking stone. If using a sheet pan, place the pan with the breads on it directly into the oven on the middle shelf.

Bake for 25 to 30 minutes. Most home ovens bake unevenly, so you may need to turn the breads after 15 minutes. When fully baked, remove the breads from the oven and place on a cooling rack.

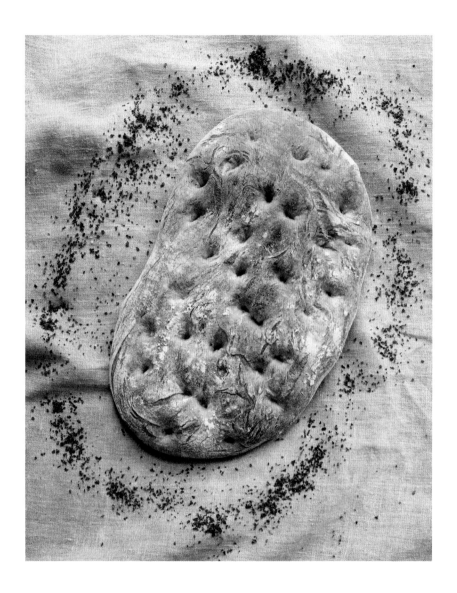

Maine Coast Focaccia

YIELDS 2 OVAL OR 1 RECTANGULAR FOCACCIA(S)

One day many years ago, as I was driving down east to Mount Desert Island to visit some of our accounts, I began musing about ingredients that are grown locally and would lend a distinctive regional character to a Maine bread. In a eureka moment, the ingredient that came to mind that day was seaweed! A number of edible seaweeds grow on the coast of Maine, including kelp, dulse, and laver. I found I could get samples of all three seaweeds in flake form from Maine Coast Sea Vegetables in Franklin and quickly started experimenting with them in breads. I ruled out kelp, as it takes on a mucilaginous quality when used in bread dough. Of the other two I thought the dulse had a clean, briny, oceanic flavor that was a great complement to the fermentation flavors found in sourdough breads. This focaccia was the first bread I developed using the dulse flakes and is a fabulous bread to serve with fish chowder or for soaking up the broth in steamed mussels.

If the idea of delicious lobster on a gummy, tasteless white hot dog roll makes you retch, try using this focaccia to fashion a wonderful if unconventional lobster roll. Cut the focaccia into wedges and then cut each wedge in half horizontally. Toast or grill with a little butter, and they are ready to be filled. Another option is to try this with the Lobster Chèvre Pâté (see recipe on page 112).

Recipe

Sourdough Starter	GRAMS	OUNCES	VOLUME
FLOUR	154	5.4	1 CUP + 1 TSP
WATER	154	5.4	⅔ CUP + 1 TBSP
WHITE SOURDOUGH MOTHER	46	1.6	¼ CUP
TOTAL	354	12.4	

Dough	GRAMS	OUNCES	VOLUME
BREAD FLOUR	505	17.8	3⅓ CUPS
WHOLE WHEAT FLOUR	91	3.2	⅓ CUP
WHITE SOURDOUGH STARTER	303	10.7	1½ CUPS
WATER	387	13.7	1¾ CUPS
OLIVE OIL	48	3.8	¼ CUP
DULSE (SEAWEED)	12	0.4	4 TBSP
SALT	15	0.5	1 TBSP
TOTAL	1,361	50.1	

Topping: sea salt or smoked salt, ¼ teaspoon per focaccia

Procedure

MIX THE SOURDOUGH STARTER

Measure the ingredients for the sourdough starter into a bowl, and with a spatula or whisk mix vigorously until the ingredients have been uniformly combined with no lumps remaining. The sourdough temperature when mixed should be between 72°F and 80°F. Let ferment until fully developed, approximately 10 to 12 hours.

MEASURE AND MIX THE DOUGH

Measure out the salt and set aside. Measure into a large bowl the bread flour, whole wheat flour, sourdough starter, water, olive oil, and dulse. Using a spatula or plastic scraper, mix the ingredients together until evenly incorporated into a ball of dough. The dough temperature should be between 70°F and 80°F. Make sure to save the leftover sourdough starter to use as a sourdough mother in later bakes!

REST AND ADD SALT

Cover the bowl with a damp cloth and let the dough rest for 30 minutes. After the dough has rested, leave the dough in the bowl and sprinkle half the salt over the dough, then flip it over and sprinkle the rest of the salt over the other side. Leaving the dough in the bowl, gently knead the salt into the dough until it is fully incorporated.

KNEAD

Turn the dough out onto a lightly floured work surface and knead until the gluten is fully developed. As you knead, you may need to lightly dust your work surface with flour occasionally to stop the dough from sticking. If the dough tightens up so that it is not easily kneaded without shredding the surface of the dough, cover it with the mixing bowl and let it rest for 3 to 5 minutes, during which time the dough will relax and become workable again. Continue kneading until the dough is supple and smooth.

FIRST RISE

Place the dough back in the bowl and cover the bowl with a damp cloth. Let the dough rise for a half hour. Again remove it from the bowl and gently stretch and fold the dough. Place the dough back in the bowl, cover, and let rise until fully proofed. Use the poke test to ascertain when to shape the dough.

PORTION AND SHAPE

There is enough dough to fill a half sheet pan (12 × 17 inches) or to make two 24-ounce oval focaccias. If making ovals, divide the dough into two equal pieces and pre-shape into two loosely formed rounds. Let dough rest for 10 minutes, then gently stretch each piece into an oval 12 inches long and 8 inches wide. Place on sheet pans that have been dusted with cornmeal or semolina. If making a rectangular focaccia, place a piece of parchment paper on a sheet pan with the paper extending over the sides of the pan by 3 inches. On a lightly floured work surface, gently pull and stretch the dough into a rectangular shape that is of uniform thickness and slightly smaller than the sheet pan. Transfer dough to the parchment-lined pan.

SECOND RISE AND DIMPLING

Cover the dough loosely with a damp cloth and let rise in a draft-free area. Employ the poke test to judge when the breads are ready to bake. Just before the breads are to be loaded into the oven, use your fingers or the end of a spatula handle to dimple the focaccia with eight to ten evenly spaced dimples on each oval, or sixteen to twenty evenly spaced dimples on the rectangular focaccia. If baking on a stone, dimple the dough when it is on the peel. If baking on the sheet pans the dough was rising on, dimple the dough in place. When dimpling the dough, unless it is over-proofed, press straight down to the bottom of the dough to create the dimples.

After dimpling, brush the dough with water and lightly sprinkle sea salt or smoked salt over the dough.

BAKE

The focaccias may be baked on a baking stone or on a sheet pan. If using a baking stone, 1 hour prior to baking, place your stone on the center oven shelf and, using the non-convection mode, preheat the oven to 500°F. If baking on a sheet pan, preheat the oven 20 minutes prior to the bake. Ten minutes prior to baking, place a sheet pan (one with sides) on the bottom shelf of the oven and fill with 1½ cups boiling water. Just prior to baking the breads, add more boiling water to the sheet pan. If using a baking stone, transfer the focaccia to a peel that has been lightly dusted with semolina or cornmeal and immediately peel the breads onto the baking stone. If using a sheet pan, place the pan with the breads on it directly into the oven on the middle shelf.

Bake for 25 to 30 minutes. Most home ovens bake unevenly, so you may need to turn the breads after 15 minutes. When fully baked, remove the breads from the oven and place on a cooling rack.

TRADITIONAL BROWN BREAD

YIELDS 1 LOAF

Steamed breads have been part of New England's culinary landscape since Native Americans taught the pilgrims how to grow corn. These breads are leavened with baking soda and are the original no-knead breads. Because they are not leavened with yeast, they do not require wheat gluten to provide the structure of the bread. Hence they provide a perfect opportunity to showcase some of the other grains commonly grown on Maine farms, such as flint corn, buckwheat, oats, barley, and rye, which contain little or no gluten.

Unlike almost all the other breads in this book, steamed breads typically contain a sweetener such as maple syrup, honey, or molasses to balance the tartness provided by the buttermilk. These breads are incredibly moist, somewhat crumbly in texture, and toast up beautifully. Steamed breads were traditionally cooked in old tin cans. Because today's can linings often include the chemical bisphenyl A (BPA), a hormone disruptor, rather than use cans for these breads I have chosen to cook the breads in pudding molds, which are BPA free and lend the breads a greatly enhanced appearance!

Like many New Englanders I have had my share of brown bread, mostly in the form of B&M Boston brown bread, at best a pedestrian example of this type of bread compared to what you can easily make at home. I did find a delicious brown bread when I was attending Bates College in Lewiston, Maine, in the late 1970s. At the time, I was living off campus and on a very tight budget. I found that Grant's Bakery, just a five-minute walk from the campus, offered a loaf of brown bread and a pint of baked beans every Saturday for a modest price. It soon became my weekly Saturday dinner along with a refreshing bottle of Narragansett beer. I am happy to say that Grant's Bakery still produces brown bread and baked beans every week from their location on Sabattus Street in Lewiston. Should you find yourself in that neck of the woods on a Saturday, I highly recommend a visit!

For your own recipe, use an unsulfured molasses. I prefer to use the regular variety rather than blackstrap in this recipe, as it does not overpower the flavor of the grains.

Recipe

Batter

	GRAMS	OUNCES	VOLUME
WHOLE WHEAT FLOUR	100	4	⅔ CUP
WHOLE RYE FLOUR	85	3	⅔ CUP
FLINT CORNMEAL	90	3	⅔ CUP
BAKING SODA	3	0.1	1 TSP
SALT	3	0.1	1 TSP
BUTTERMILK	227	8	1 CUP
MOLASSES, UNSULFURED	160	6	½ CUP
TOTAL	668	24.2	

Procedure

PREP

Butter the inside of a 1½-quart pudding mold. Choose a deep pot that will accommodate the pudding mold. Place a canning lid, metal rack, or some other heat-safe object under the mold in the pot to prevent scorching due to direct contact between the pudding mold and the pot bottom. Fill the pot with enough water to come three-quarters of the way up the side of the pudding mold. On the stovetop bring the water to a slow simmer.

MEASURE AND MIX THE DOUGH

Measure the dry ingredients into a mixing bowl and briefly whisk to distribute evenly. In another bowl, whisk together the buttermilk and molasses. Add the wet mixture to the dry ingredients and stir with a spatula until the dry ingredients are evenly incorporated into the wet ones. Pour the batter into the pudding mold and secure the cover on the mold. If a cover is unavailable, use aluminum foil; secure the foil to the mold with a piece of string around the rim.

COOK

Place the pudding mold into the pot of simmering water. Ensure that the water comes three-quarters of the way up the sides of the pudding mold. Place a lid on the pot and continue to simmer slowly. Steam the brown bread for a total of 1½ hours. After 45 minutes, top the water in the pot so that it remains three-quarters of the way up the side of the pudding mold. When done, remove the pudding mold from the pot and remove the lid from the mold. Insert a thin skewer into the bread; the skewer should come out clean. The internal temperature of the bread should reach 200°F when fully cooked. Flip the loaf out onto a cooling rack (it should come out of the mold easily). Let the bread cool to room temperature before slicing.

ABENAKI FLINT CORN BREAD

YIELDS 1 LOAF

This bread highlights the extraordinary flavor of the Abenaki flint corn grown in Unity, Maine, at Songbird Farm by Johanna Davis and Adam Nordell. The depth and complexity of flavor is remarkable, particularly when tasted side by side with the de-germed cornmeal available in most supermarkets. If you do not have access to a stone-ground flint cornmeal, any whole cornmeal will work in this recipe.

Maple syrups are graded by taste and color, and the grading nomenclature has changed in the past couple of years. I like to use Grade B maple syrup or what is now called "Grade A: dark color and robust flavor" in this recipe. The more assertive flavor balances the bitterness introduced by the whole wheat flour.

If you want an enlightening demonstration on the importance of ingredient selection, make two of these corn breads, one with stone-ground whole flint corn and real maple syrup and the other with de-germed cornmeal (Quaker Oats is the most common brand) and imitation maple syrup. Taste side by side and you will easily see how choosing higher-quality, natural, and less processed ingredients translates to a bread that tastes better and is more nutritious!

Recipe

Batter

	GRAMS	OUNCES	VOLUME
WHOLE WHEAT FLOUR	158	5.6	1 CUP
FLINT CORNMEAL	156	5.5	1 CUP
BAKING SODA	3	0.1	1 TSP
SALT	3	0.1	1 TSP
BUTTERMILK	256	9.0	⅓ CUP
PURE MAPLE SYRUP	102	3.6	⅓ CUP
TOTAL	678	23.9	

Procedure

PREP

Butter the inside of a 1½-quart pudding mold. Choose a deep pot that will accommodate the pudding mold. Place a canning lid, metal rack, or some other heat-safe object under the mold in the pot to prevent scorching due to direct contact between the pudding mold and the pot bottom. Fill the pot with enough water to come three-quarters of the way up the side of the pudding mold. On the stovetop bring the water to a slow simmer.

MEASURE AND MIX THE DOUGH

Measure the dry ingredients into a mixing bowl and briefly whisk to distribute evenly. In another bowl, whisk together the buttermilk and maple syrup. Add the wet mixture to the dry ingredients and stir with a spatula until the dry ingredients are evenly incorporated into the wet ones. Pour the batter into the pudding mold and secure the cover on the mold. If a cover is unavailable, use aluminum foil; secure the foil to the mold with a piece of string around the rim.

COOK

Place the pudding mold into the pot of simmering water. Ensure that the water comes three-quarters of the way up the sides of the pudding mold. Place a lid on the pot and continue to simmer slowly. Steam the bread for a total of 1½ hours. After 45 minutes, top the water in the pot so that it remains three-quarters of the way up the side of the pudding mold. When done, remove the pudding mold from the pot and remove the lid from the mold. Insert a thin skewer into the bread; the skewer should come out clean. The internal temperature of the bread should reach 200°F when fully cooked. Flip the loaf out onto a cooling rack (it should come out of the mold easily). Let the bread cool to room temperature before slicing.

PUMPKIN BREAD

YIELDS 1 LOAF

This is not your typical pumpkin bread! These days, "pumpkin" refers as often to the spices used in pumpkin pie—cinnamon, allspice, and clove—as to the actual squash variety. If you choose to use fresh pumpkin for this recipe, make sure it is specifically grown for cooking and baking purposes and not for use as a jack-o-lantern. Many other common squashes such as butternut and acorn will work just as well. The squash flavor is not dominating but complements the grains nicely.

Rather than the typical pumpkin pie spices, I season this bread with sumac berry powder, which is sold by Gryffon Ridge Spice Merchants in Litchfield, and SKORDO in Freeport and Portland, Maine. While their sumac berries do not come from Maine, you could forage for the berries of the staghorn sumac (Rhus typhina), which is a native of Maine, and use those just as successfully. Sumac berries have an astringent, tart flavor due to the presence of malic, gallic, and tannic acids. This bread is more savory than sweet, particularly when compared to steamed brown bread.

Recipe

Prep

Prep	GRAMS	OUNCES	VOLUME
HULLED PUMPKIN SEEDS (PEPITAS)	45	1.6	⅓ CUP
PUMPKIN	161	5.7	⅔ CUP

Batter

Batter	GRAMS	OUNCES	VOLUME
BARLEY FLOUR	107	3.8	¾ CUPS
BUCKWHEAT FLOUR	64	2.3	⅓ CUP + 1 TBSP
FLINT CORNMEAL	48	1.7	⅓ CUP
SUMAC BERRIES	11	0.4	2 TBSP
PUMPKIN SEEDS (PEPITAS)	45	1.6	⅓ CUP
BAKING SODA	3	0.1	1 TSP
SALT	4	0.1	1 TSP
PUREED PUMPKIN	161	5.7	⅔ CUP
MAPLE SYRUP	118	4.2	½ CUP + 1 TSP
BUTTERMILK	143	5.0	⅔ CUP
TOTAL	704	24.9	

PREP

Preheat the oven to 350°F. Cut a small pumpkin or squash in half and scoop out the seeds. Place halves cut side down on a greased roasting pan, then pour a cup of water into the pan. Place in the oven and cook until tender, approximately 30 to 45 minutes depending on the size of the pumpkin or squash. Cool slightly and scoop out the flesh. Measure out the amount needed and puree using a blender or food processor.

Heavily butter the inside of a 1½-quart pudding mold. Measure out the pumpkin seeds, put them into the mold, and roll them around the mold until the bottom and sides are evenly coated with seeds.

Choose a deep pot that will accommodate the pudding mold. Place a canning lid, metal rack, or some other heat-safe object under the mold in the pot to prevent scorching due to direct contact between the pudding mold and the pot bottom. Fill the pot with enough water to come three-quarters of the way up the side of the pudding mold. On the stovetop bring the water to a slow simmer.

MEASURE AND MIX THE DOUGH

Measure the dry ingredients into a mixing bowl and briefly whisk to distribute evenly. In another bowl, whisk together the pumpkin puree, maple syrup, and buttermilk. Add the wet mixture to the dry ingredients and stir with a spatula until the dry ingredients are evenly incorporated into the wet ones. Pour the batter into the pudding mold and secure the cover on the mold. If a cover is unavailable, use aluminum foil; secure the foil to the mold with a piece of string around the rim.

COOK

Place the pudding mold into the pot of simmering water. Ensure that the water comes three-quarters of the way up the sides of the pudding mold. Place a lid on the pot and continue to simmer slowly. Steam the bread for a total of 1½ hours. After 45 minutes, top the water in the pot so that it remains three-quarters of the way up the side of the pudding mold. When done, remove the pudding mold from the pot and remove the lid from the mold. Insert a thin skewer into the bread; the skewer should come out clean. The internal temperature of the bread should reach 200°F when fully cooked. Flip the loaf out onto a cooling rack (it should come out of the mold easily). Let the bread cool to room temperature before slicing.

BUCKWHEAT BREAD

YIELDS 1 LOAF

The buckwheat flour used in this recipe is the same used to make ployes, a delicious pancake that originally was a staple in the Acadian kitchens of the Saint John River valley in northernmost Maine. This variety, Tatary buckwheat (Fagopyrum tatari-

cum), differs from common or Japanese buckwheat (Fagopyrum esculentum) that is most commonly sold as buckwheat flour. Buckwheats are gluten free, and this bread, if made with gluten-free oats, is the only gluten-free recipe in the book.

Juniper berries are the primary ingredient that gives gin its distinct flavor. In this bread they lend an intriguing, aromatic note.

Recipe

Batter	GRAMS	OUNCES	VOLUME
BUCKWHEAT FLOUR	120	4.2	1 CUP
FLINT CORNMEAL	75	2.6	¾ CUP
ROLLED OATS	75	2.6	1 CUP
JUNIPER BERRIES	3	0.1	1 TBSP
SALT	4	0.1	1½ TSP
BAKING SODA	4	0.1	1½ TSP
MAPLE SYRUP	98	3.4	⅓ CUP
BUTTERMILK	300	10.6	1¾ CUPS
TOTAL	679	23.7	

PREP

Preheat the oven to 300°F. Measure out the oats and spread them evenly on a sheet pan. Bake for 8 minutes to toast. Mince the juniper berries.

Butter the inside of a 1½-quart pudding mold. Choose a deep pot that will accommodate the pudding mold. Place a canning lid, metal rack, or some other heat-safe object under the mold in the pot to prevent scorching due to direct contact between the pudding mold and the pot bottom. Fill the pot with enough water to come three-quarters of the way up the side of the pudding mold. On the stovetop bring the water to a slow simmer.

MEASURE AND MIX THE DOUGH

Measure the dry ingredients into a mixing bowl and briefly whisk to distribute evenly. In another bowl, whisk together the maple syrup and buttermilk. Add the wet mixture to the dry ingredients and stir with a spatula until the dry ingredients have been evenly incorporated into the wet ones. Pour the batter into the pudding mold and secure the cover on the mold. If a cover is unavailable, use aluminum foil; secure the foil to the mold with a piece of string around the rim.

COOK

Place the pudding mold into the pot of simmering water. Ensure that the water comes three-quarters of the way up the sides of the pudding mold. Place a lid on the pot and continue to simmer slowly. Steam the bread for a total of 1½ hours. After 45 minutes, top the water in the pot up so that it remains three-quarters of the way up the side of the pudding mold. When done, remove the pudding mold from the pot and remove the lid from the mold. Insert a thin skewer into the bread; the skewer should come out clean. The internal temperature of the bread should reach 200°F when fully cooked. Flip the loaf out onto a cooling rack (it should come out of the mold easily). Let the bread cool to room temperature before slicing.

SOURDOUGH BAGELS

YIELDS 12 BAGELS

A few years after Borealis Breads opened, there was a brief bagel boom in Maine; it seemed bagel cafes and bagel wholesalers were popping up everywhere. Whether retail or wholesale, any bakery startup is a precarious venture. The bagel boom came and went, and most of the bagel enterprises closed, but today bagels are making a comeback. You can find great bagels at Scratch Baking Co. in South Portland, at Forage Market in Lewiston, or even at the County Co-op in Houlton, where they offer bagels made by Sara Williams of Aurora Mills and Farm. Local farmers' markets are also a good place to check for handcrafted bagels—Hootenanny Bakery provides some of the mid-coast markets with tasty, chewy bagels. The rest of us search for a real bagel in the great swaths of rural Maine. Usually all that can be found are frozen par-baked imposters that rise from the dead in the convection ovens of convenience stores, or the "bread products" at Dunkin Donuts that look like bagels but are insipid shadows of the real thing.

Fortunately, truly delicious bagels are not difficult to make, though they do demand time and patience. Bagel doughs are stiffer than any of the other doughs in this book, so don't be surprised at the amount of work it takes to incorporate all the flour into the dough. Unlike most commercial bagels, which are baked in steam-injected ovens, an authentic bagel is briefly placed in boiling water prior to baking. This gelatinizes the starches in the bagel crust and, along with the 500°F baking temperature, helps to create the signature crispy crust of a great bagel. You will need a large pot big enough to boil two to four bagels at a time and a large slotted spoon or wide spatula to remove the bagels from the boiling water. Another key to developing the flavor found in great bagels is to retard them (using cold temperatures to significantly slow down the fermentation) in the refrigerator overnight before boiling and baking them. Each of the three bagel recipes here rely on these techniques, and for your effort and patience will yield a dozen superb bagels.

This recipe is the perfect illustration of how a simple formula can create an incredibly appealing and versatile food. Four ingredients—no fruit, nuts, cheese, oils, herbs—just a simple dough that is transformed through fermentation and an unusual production technique into a perfect blend of taste and texture. Bagels are traditionally leavened with yeast cakes or dried yeast. I have departed from that custom. As with almost all the recipes in this book, these bagels are leavened with a sourdough starter. The rye sourdough starter lends an earthy, tangy flavor to these scrumptious bagels. Mix these the night before, retard overnight, and in less than an hour the next morning you can have bagels fresh from the oven.

Recipe

Rye Sourdough Starter	GRAMS	OUNCES	VOLUME
WHOLE RYE FLOUR	163	5.8	1⅓ CUPS
WATER	106	3.7	½ CUP
WHOLE WHEAT SOURDOUGH MOTHER	41	1.4	¼ CUP
TOTAL	310	10.9	

Dough	GRAMS	OUNCES	VOLUME
BREAD FLOUR	1,021	36.0	6¾ CUPS
RYE SOURDOUGH STARTER	255	9.0	1⅛ CUPS
WATER	572	20.2	2½ CUPS + 3 TBSP
SALT	24	0.8	1 TBSP + 2 TSP
TOTAL	1,872	66	

Optional toppings: sesame seeds (hulled or unhulled), poppy seeds, dried chopped onion or garlic (rehydrated)

Procedure

MIX THE RYE SOURDOUGH STARTER

Measure the ingredients for the sourdough starter into a bowl and mix until they come together to form a uniform ball of dough. Because of the presence of rye flour in this starter, the dough will be quite sticky compared to the ones with all white or whole wheat starter. The dough temperature when mixed should be between 72°F and 80°F. Let rest for 6 to 8 hours. When fully fermented the starter will have expanded in size, show some cracks on the surface, and have softened up. It will not spring back when poked, as the rye flour does not provide the elasticity that wheat flour does.

MEASURE AND MIX THE DOUGH

Measure into a large bowl the flour, rye sourdough starter, water, and salt. Start mixing using a spatula or plastic scraper. When most but not all the flour has been incorporated into the dough, leave the dough in the bowl and use your hands to knead until all the flour is incorporated. The dough temperature should be between 70°F and 80°F. Make sure to save the leftover sourdough starter to use as a sourdough mother in later bakes!

KNEAD

Turn the dough out onto a lightly floured work surface and knead. The dough should be quite stiff. As you knead the dough, be careful not to shred the strands of gluten that are developing. If the dough does become too tight and starts to shred, stop and cover it with the mixing bowl. Let it rest for 5 minutes before resuming the kneading. You may need to let the dough rest several times before the kneading has fully developed the gluten. Continue kneading until the dough is supple and smooth.

FIRST RISE

Place the dough back in the bowl and cover the bowl with a damp cloth. Let the dough rise until fully proofed. Use the poke test to ascertain when to shape the dough.

SHAPE THE BAGELS

Remove the dough from the bowl and scale into twelve 5-ounce pieces that are squarish in shape. Flatten each piece of dough and roll it into a cylinder, then roll the cylinder back and forth with both hands until it is 9 to 10 inches long and an even diameter along its full length. Wrap the cylinder around your palm and let the two ends overlap by 2 inches or so. Turn your palm down and roll the overlapped ends on the work surface until they are joined and you have a circular piece of dough with an even diameter all the way around. Place the finished bagels on a sheet pan that has been dusted with semolina or cornmeal. Leave about 3 inches of space between the bagels so they do not proof into each other.

SECOND RISE

Cover the bagels with a damp cloth and let rise in a draft-free spot for 20 to 30 minutes. To test if the bagels are ready to be put in the refrigerator overnight, fill a medium-size bowl with water and place a bagel in the water. If the bagel sinks to the bottom and does not rise back to the top after a few seconds, then the bagels need to proof longer. If the bagel rises to the surface, they are ready to be refrigerated. Cover the pan of bagels loosely with a plastic bag and refrigerate overnight.

BOIL, TOP, AND BAKE

In the morning preheat the oven to 500°F. Fill a large, wide pot three-quarters full of water. Add 2 tablespoons malt syrup or honey to the water and bring to a boil. While waiting for the water to boil, choose which toppings, if any, you would like to use. Place ¼ cup of each out on small plates. Next to the toppings, place a sheet pan lined with parchment paper. (A 12 × 17-inch sheet pan will accommodate six bagels.)

Remove the bagels from the refrigerator. Once the water is boiling, drop two or three bagels top down into the water. Boil the bagels for 45 to 60 seconds, then, using a large slotted spoon or spatula, flip them over and boil for another 45 to 60 seconds. Remove bagels from the water and place on an extra sheet pan. When all the bagels are boiled, starting with the ones boiled first (the coolest ones), place each bagel top down on the topping of your choice. Flip the bagel over and place top side up on the sheet pan lined with parchment.

Place the bagels in the oven and bake for 10 minutes, then rotate each pan of bagels to ensure an even bake. Continue to bake for an additional 10 to 12 minutes. Remove the pans from the oven and place on a cooling rack. If after baking bagels the first time you find the bottoms are too dark, in the future you can "double pan" the bagels to avoid burning the bottoms before the tops have colored properly. To "double pan" the bagels, nest the pan of bagels that are ready for the oven on top of a similar-size pan to provide additional thermal insulation and then bake as described.

MAINE MULTIGRAIN BAGELS

YIELDS 12 BAGELS

When I see "flavored" bagels, ones where nontraditional ingredients such as pesto, jalapeño-cheddar, or blueberry have been added to the bagel dough, I usually flee in a hurry. I would rather get creative with the bagel spreads than with the dough. Where I do deviate from tradition is in the use of other grains and flours, as I do in this recipe and in the Whole Grain Spelt Bagel recipe. With a panoply of Maine grains, wheat, rye, rolled oats, and flint cornmeal, these bagels are bursting with grainy goodness!

Recipe

Rye Sourdough Starter	GRAMS	OUNCES	VOLUME	BAKER'S %
WHOLE RYE FLOUR	159	5.6	1⅓ CUPS	100.00%
WATER	104	3.7	½ CUP	65.00%
WHOLE WHEAT SOURDOUGH MOTHER	48	1.7	¼ CUP	30.00%
TOTAL	311	11		

Prep Oat Mash	GRAMS	OUNCES	VOLUME	BAKER'S %
OATS	37	1.3	⅓ CUP	
WATER	56	2.0	¼ CUP	
TOTAL	93	3.3		

Prep Corn Mash	GRAMS	OUNCES	VOLUME	BAKER'S %
CORNMEAL	22	0.8	⅛ CUP	
WATER	87	3.1	⅓ CUP + 1 TBSP	
AFTER COOKING	93	3.3		

Dough	GRAMS	OUNCES	VOLUME	BAKER'S %
BREAD FLOUR	797	28.1	5⅓ CUPS	85.76%
WHOLE WHEAT FLOUR	132	4.7	¾ CUP + 2 TBSP	14.24%
WATER	474	16.7	2⅛ CUPS + 1 TBSP	51.00%
RYE SOURDOUGH STARTER	260	9.2	2⅓ CUPS	28.00%
CORN MASH	93	3.3	⅓ CUP + 1 TBSP	10.00%
TOASTED OAT MASH	93	3.3	⅓ CUP + 2 TBSP	10.00%
SALT	22	0.8	1 TBSP + 1 TSP	2.34%
TOTAL	1,871	66.1		

Optional toppings: sesame seeds (hulled or unhulled), poppy seeds, dried chopped onion or garlic (rehydrated)

Procedure

MIX THE RYE SOURDOUGH STARTER

Measure into a bowl the ingredients for the rye sourdough starter and mix until they come together to form a uniform ball of dough. Because of the presence of rye flour in this starter, the dough will be quite sticky compared to the ones with all white or whole wheat starter. The dough temperature when mixed should be between 72°F and 80°F. Let rest for 6 to 8 hours. When fully fermented the starter will have expanded in size, show some cracks on the surface, and have softened up. It will not spring back when poked, as the rye flour does not provide the elasticity that wheat flour does.

PREP

Preheat the oven to 300°F. Measure out the oats and spread them evenly on a sheet pan. Bake for 8 to 10 minutes. Place the toasted oats in a bowl and pour the boiling water over them. Stir and let sit, but do not add to the dough until oats have cooled to room temperature.

Place the cornmeal and water in a heavy-bottomed saucepan and let simmer slowly at a very low heat, stirring the cornmeal every 5 minutes to ensure it does not stick to the bottom of the pan. When done, the corn mash should be soft and not gritty. It's a good idea to taste it to be sure the consistency is correct. Remove from the heat and let cool to room temperature before adding to the dough.

MEASURE AND MIX THE DOUGH

Measure all the ingredients into a large bowl. Start mixing using a spatula or plastic scraper. When most but not all the flour has been incorporated into the dough, leave the dough in the bowl and use your hands to knead until all the flour is incorporated. The dough temperature should be between 70°F and 80°F. Make sure to save the leftover sourdough starter to use as a sourdough mother in later bakes!

KNEAD

Turn the dough out onto a lightly floured work surface and knead. The dough should be quite stiff. As you knead the dough, be careful not to shred the strands of gluten that are developing. If the dough does become too tight and starts to shred, stop and cover it with the mixing bowl. Let it rest for 5 minutes before resuming the kneading. You may need to let the dough rest several times before the kneading has fully developed the gluten. Continue kneading until the dough is supple and smooth.

FIRST RISE

Place the dough back in the bowl and cover the bowl with a damp cloth. Let the dough rise until fully proofed. Use the poke test to ascertain when to shape the dough.

SHAPE THE BAGELS

Remove the dough from the bowl and scale into twelve 5-ounce pieces that are squarish in shape. Flatten each piece of dough and roll it into a cylinder, then roll the cylinder back and forth with both hands until it is 9 to 10 inches long and an even diameter along its full length. Wrap the cylinder around your palm and let the two ends overlap by 2 inches or so. Turn your palm down and roll the overlapped ends on the work surface until they are joined and you have a circular piece of dough with an even diameter all the way around. Place the finished bagels on a sheet pan that has been dusted with semolina or cornmeal. Leave about 3 inches of space between the bagels so they do not proof into each other.

SECOND RISE

Cover the bagels with a damp cloth and let rise in a draft-free spot for 20 to 30 minutes. To test if the bagels are ready to be put in the refrigerator overnight, fill a medium-size bowl with water and place a bagel in the water. If the bagel sinks to the bottom and does not rise back to the top after a few seconds, then the bagels need to proof longer. If the bagel rises to the surface, they are ready to be refrigerated. Cover the pan of bagels with a plastic bag and refrigerate overnight.

BOIL, TOP, AND BAKE

In the morning preheat the oven to 500°F. Fill a large, wide pot three-quarters full of water. Add 2 tablespoons malt syrup or honey to the water and bring to a boil. While waiting for the water to boil, choose which toppings, if any, you would like to use. Place ¼ cup of each out on small plates. Next to the toppings, place a sheet pan lined with parchment paper. (A 12 × 17-inch sheet pan will accommodate six bagels.)

Remove the bagels from the refrigerator. Once the water is boiling, drop two or three bagels top down into the water. Boil the bagels for 45 to 60 seconds, then, using a large slotted spoon or spatula, flip them over and boil for another 45 to 60 seconds. Remove bagels from the water and place on an extra sheet pan. When all the bagels are boiled, starting with the ones boiled first (the coolest ones), place each bagel top down on a topping of your choice. Flip the bagel over and place top side up on the sheet pan lined with parchment.

Place the bagels in the oven and bake for 10 minutes, then rotate each pan of bagels to ensure an even bake. Continue to bake for an additional 10 to 12 minutes. Remove the pans from the oven and place on a cooling rack. If after baking bagels the first time you find the bottoms are too dark, in the future you can "double pan" the bagels to avoid burning the bottoms before the tops have colored properly. To "double pan" the bagels, nest the pan of bagels that are ready for the oven on top of a similar-size pan to provide additional thermal insulation and then bake as described.

WHOLE GRAIN SPELT BAGELS

YIELDS 12 BAGELS

I first came across bagels made with spelt flour in 2006 when I provided a bit of advice and a huge portion of encouragement to my fellow Bates graduates Beth George and Tim Kane. They were starting Spelt Right Foods, a wholesale bakery in Yarmouth, Maine, specializing in the production of bagels made with 100 percent spelt flour. My recipe contains about a 50/50 blend of spelt flour and wheat flour. For bagel lovers who like to eschew the use of white bread flour, these bagels, a blend of whole spelt flour, whole wheat flour, and sifted wheat flour, are a chewy toothsome delight. The spelt flour lacks the slightly bitter bite of whole wheat flour and lends these bagels a nice mellow flavor.

Recipe

Sourdough Starter

	GRAMS	OUNCES	VOLUME
WHOLE WHEAT FLOUR	175	6.2	1⅛ CUPS
WATER	105	3.7	½ CUP
WHOLE WHEAT SOURDOUGH MOTHER	53	1.9	¼ CUP
TOTAL	333	11.8	

Dough

	GRAMS	OUNCES	VOLUME
WHOLE SPELT FLOUR	605	21.3	5 CUPS + 1 TBSP
SIFTED WHOLE WHEAT FLOUR	405	14.3	2⅔ CUPS
WHOLE WHEAT SOURDOUGH STARTER	283	10.0	1½ CUPS
WATER	556	19.6	2⅛ CUPS + 1 TBSP
SALT	24	0.8	1 TBSP + 2 TSP
TOTAL	1,872	66	

Optional toppings: sesame seeds (hulled or un-hulled), poppy seeds, dried chopped onion or garlic (rehydrated)

Procedure

MIX THE SOURDOUGH STARTER

Measure the ingredients for the sourdough starter into a bowl and mix until they come together to form a uniform ball of dough. If you're using rye flour in your starter, the dough will be quite sticky compared to those with all white or whole wheat starter. The dough temperature when mixed should be between

72°F and 80°F. Let rest for 6 to 8 hours. When fully fermented the starter will have expanded in size, show some cracks on the surface, and have softened up. It will not spring back when poked, as the rye flour does not provide the elasticity that wheat flour does.

MEASURE AND MIX THE DOUGH

Measure into a large bowl the flours, whole wheat sourdough starter, water, and salt. Start mixing using a spatula or plastic scraper. When most but not all the flour has been incorporated into the dough, leave the dough in the bowl and use your hands to knead until all the flour is incorporated. The dough temperature should be between 70°F and 80°F. Make sure to save the leftover sourdough starter to use as a sourdough mother in later bakes!

KNEAD

Turn the dough out onto a lightly floured work surface and knead. The dough should be quite stiff. As you knead the dough, be careful not to shred the strands of gluten that are developing. If the dough does become too tight and starts to shred, stop and cover it with the mixing bowl. Let it rest for 5 minutes before resuming the kneading. You may need to let the dough rest several times before the kneading has fully developed the gluten. Continue kneading until the dough is supple and smooth.

FIRST RISE

Place the dough back in the bowl and cover the bowl with a damp cloth. Let the dough rise until fully proofed. Use the poke test to ascertain when to shape the dough.

SHAPE THE BAGELS

Remove the dough from the bowl and scale into twelve 5-ounce pieces that are squarish in shape. Flatten each piece of dough and roll it into a cylinder, then roll the cylinder back and forth with both hands until it is 9 to 10 inches long and of an even diameter along its full length. Wrap the cylinder around your palm and let the two ends overlap by 2 inches or so. Turn your palm down and roll the over-lapped ends on the work surface until they are joined and you have a circular piece of dough with an even diameter all the way around. Place the finished bagels on a sheet pan that has been dusted with semolina or cornmeal. Leave about 3 inches of space between the bagels so they do not proof into each other.

SECOND RISE

Cover the bagels with a damp cloth and let rise in a draft-free spot for 20 to 30 minutes. To test if the bagels are ready to be put in the refrigerator overnight, fill a medium-size bowl with water and place a bagel in the water. If the bagel sinks to the bottom and does not rise back to the top after a few seconds, then the bagels need to proof longer. If the bagel rises to the surface, they are ready to be refrigerated. Cover the pan of bagels loosely with a plastic bag and refrigerate overnight.

BOIL, TOP, AND BAKE

In the morning preheat the oven to 500°F. Fill a large, wide pot three-quarters full of water. Add 2 tablespoons malt syrup or honey to the water and bring to a boil. While waiting for the water to boil, choose which toppings, if any, you would like to use. Place ¼ cup of each out on small plates. Next to the toppings, place a sheet pan lined with parchment paper. (A 12 × 17-inch sheet pan will accommodate six bagels.)

Remove the bagels from the refrigerator. Once the water is boiling, drop two to three bagels top down into the water. Boil the bagels for 45 to 60 seconds, then, using a large slotted spoon or spatula, flip them over and boil for another 45 to 60 seconds. Remove bagels from the water and place on an extra sheet pan. When all the bagels are boiled, starting with the ones boiled first (the coolest ones), place each bagel top down on the topping of your choice. Flip the bagel over and place top side up on the sheet pan lined with parchment.

Place the bagels in the oven and bake for 10 minutes, then rotate each pan of bagels to ensure an even bake. Continue to bake for an additional 10 to 12 minutes. Remove the pans from the oven and place on a cooling rack. If after baking bagels the first time you find the bottoms are too dark, in the future you can "double pan" the bagels to avoid burning the bottoms before the tops have colored properly. To "double pan" the bagels, nest the pan of bagels that are ready for the oven on top of a similar-size pan to provide additional thermal insulation and then bake as described.

Glorious slices of sourdough are decorated here with bright, creamy, herbaceous, and earthy elements that add a fourth dimension to a sandwich.

BEYOND THE BREAD—SPREADS AND FILLINGS

SPRING EDAMAME HUMMUS

MAKES 3 CUPS

Fresh, bright green, and full of flavor, this hummus is different than any you've had before. Made with peas and edamame (young soybeans), the flavor is highlighted with lime and tahini. I love using fresh snow peas or chunks of crusty bread as the vehicle. Perfect in a veggie sandwich!

2 cloves garlic, peeled and crushed

4 tablespoons fresh lime juice

2 cups cooked shelled edamame

1 cup fresh peas, blanched

1½ tablespoons sesame tahini

1 tablespoon ground cumin

2 tablespoons chopped fresh parsley

1 teaspoon salt

¼ teaspoon cayenne pepper or white pepper

1 tablespoon hot sauce

In the bowl of a food processor, place the crushed cloves of garlic and lime juice. Pulse until the garlic is minced.

Add the edamame and fresh peas, tahini, cumin, parsley, salt, pepper, and hot sauce.

Process until smooth, scraping down the sides often to incorporate the ingredients. Add a tablespoon or two of water or olive oil, if necessary, to make a smooth paste. Adjust the pepper and salt to your taste.

Serve with fresh snow peas and/or chunks of crusty whole grain bread.

MANGO HUMMUS

MAKES 2½ CUPS

This makes a nice-size batch that will keep for several days in the refrigerator. It has a fruity, nutty flavor that tastes fresh and light! It's great on veggie sandwiches with shredded carrots and arugula.

2 (15-ounce) cans garbanzo beans

1 ripe mango, peeled and pitted

Juice from 1 lemon or lime

1 clove garlic, grated

¼ cup minced fresh cilantro

½ teaspoon salt

Dash of hot pepper sauce (optional)

In a blender or food processor, combine all ingredients. Blend thoroughly until mixture is smooth. If you like a chunkier texture, puree until it is the consistency you and your family will enjoy.

ALMOND YOGURT SPREAD

MAKES 1 CUP (CAN EASILY BE DOUBLED)

This spread is easy and quick to prepare, and delicious. Make it sweeter by using vanilla yogurt or more savory with plain yogurt. It's great for dipping apples, celery, carrots, and broccoli or as a spread on your favorite sandwich.

½ cup plain or vanilla yogurt

½ cup almond butter (soy, sunflower, and peanut also work well)

Pinch of sea salt

1 teaspoon honey or maple syrup

In a small mixing bowl, combine all ingredients and mix until thoroughly incorporated. Chill until ready to serve.

TARRAGON CHICKEN SALAD

MAKES 4 MEDIUM-SIZE SANDWICHES

Business manager Kelley Sevigny developed the famous Borealis Tarragon Chicken Salad. The story behind the recipe includes an herbaceous switcheroo—parsley in an early version became tarragon one fine day—and the rest is history.

1¼ pounds cooked chicken

2 tablespoons dried or ¼ cup fresh tarragon

¾ cup chopped walnuts

1 cup mayonnaise

½ teaspoon sea salt

½ teaspoon white pepper

Separate the cooked chicken into two equal parts. Chop one half of the chicken into bite-size chunks and set aside in a large bowl.

Place the other half into a food processor. Pulse to break down the chicken into smaller pieces. Add tarragon, walnuts, and mayonnaise and pulse to create a moist, chunky chicken salad.

Remove mixture from the food processor and place into the bowl with the remaining chopped chicken. Add salt and pepper and fold together until mixture is combined.

Serve on Borealis potato bread or your favorite variety.

LOBSTER CHÈVRE PÂTÈ

MAKES 2 CUPS

This spread incorporates tangy fresh goat cheese with succulent seafood. It would be perfect on Maine Coast Focaccia (see recipe on page 82) or chilled and made into little patties. Dip the patties in beaten egg, then bread crumbs, and fry in butter until golden. Serve the crispy patties atop fresh greens for a lovely salad.

12 ounces plain fresh chèvre, room temperature

Juice of ½ lime (approximately 3 tablespoons)

3 tablespoons finely chopped fresh cilantro, chives, or parsley

Dash of sea salt

A few grinds of black pepper

6 ounces cooked lobster meat, chopped

Mash the chèvre in a shallow bowl with a fork. Stir in the lime juice, herbs, salt, and pepper. When combined, add the lobster and stir gently until completely incorporated.

Serve immediately. Or, for a fancier presentation, line a dish with plastic wrap and fill with the pâté. Fold the plastic snugly over the mixture. Cover with another layer of wrap and chill. When ready to serve, remove the top layer of plastic wrap. Unmold the pâté onto a pretty plate and gently peel back the bottom wrap to uncover the pâté. Sprinkle with more freshly chopped herbs and serve with sliced baguette. Delicious!

HOT CRABMEAT SPREAD

MAKES ABOUT 3 CUPS

This creamy spread is perfect on a slice of Borealis Multigrain Bread alongside a Caesar salad. Simple, elegant, and delicious, fresh Maine crabmeat is sweet with just a whisper of ocean breeze. Smoked trout, lobster, or salmon can be substituted here to tailor this recipe to your preference.

¾ cup sour cream

1 tablespoon grated Vidalia onion

¾ teaspoon dry mustard powder

8 ounces cream cheese

2 tablespoons fresh lemon juice

1 teaspoon Worcestershire sauce

¼ teaspoon garlic powder

1 pound fresh Maine crabmeat

½ cup shredded sharp cheddar

Paprika

Preheat the oven to 325°F.

In a large bowl, combine sour cream, onion, mustard, cream cheese, lemon juice, Worcestershire sauce, and garlic powder. Gently fold in the crabmeat and cheddar cheese.

Grease a 1½-quart casserole with vegetable spray. Spoon mixture into casserole dish and sprinkle with paprika.

Bake for 30 minutes. Serve immediately.

Kitchen Garden Spread

MAKES ABOUT 2 CUPS

This creamy spread is wonderful on bagels, on crusty bread, or on top of a warm piece of grilled steak. Using goat cheese in combination with mascarpone produces a lighter spread, just right for a warm slice of bread straight from the oven.

8 ounces mascarpone cheese

8 ounces plain chèvre

1 tablespoon chopped fresh rosemary

¼ cup minced fresh parsley

¼ cup minced fresh chives

½ teaspoon garlic powder, or 1 clove garlic, minced or grated on a microplane

½ teaspoon white pepper

½ teaspoon salt

In a medium bowl, combine all ingredients together until smooth. Chill before serving.

TIP

Note: This spread is even better the day after it's made, so the flavors can dance around a bit. If you have an herb garden and want to add oregano, thyme, marjoram, or sage, feel free to supplement the herbs to your taste.

BACON AND ROASTED-GARLIC BLUE CHEESE SPREAD

MAKES ABOUT 3 CUPS

Two ways to marry this rich, delicious spread and Borealis Breads include slicing the top two inches of a loaf, hollowing out some of the center, filling it up with creamy-bacony goodness, then broiling the topped loaf until bubbly. Our other favorite is to slather a slice of sourdough with apple butter then this savory spread. Your taste buds will tap dance!

5 slices bacon, reserving 2 tablespoons rendered bacon fat

16 ounces Neufchatel cheese

½ cup (1 stick) butter, softened

1 teaspoon salt

1 teaspoon pepper

3 tablespoons roasted garlic puree

12 ounces blue cheese, crumbled

Cook bacon until light brown and crispy. Drain on a plate lined with paper towels.

Blend together 2 tablespoons reserved bacon fat with the Neufchatel cheese and butter. Add the salt, pepper, and roasted garlic. Blend again until smooth. Crumble the crisped bacon into the cheese mixture. Add the blue cheese, mixing until well incorporated.

This spread will keep in the refrigerator for 2 to 3 days, or it can be frozen.

TO ROAST GARLIC: Cut the top quarter off a head of garlic to expose the cloves. Place in a foil-lined baking dish and drizzle heavily with olive oil. Bake for 50 minutes at 300°F. Remove from the oven and let sit until cool enough to handle. Squeeze the now very soft cloves out of the garlic skins into a dish. (Save the roasted garlic–flavored oil from the bottom of the dish to use in other recipes.) Store roasted garlic and oil in a covered jar in the refrigerator until ready to use.

SMOKED SALMON PÂTÉ

SERVES 6–8

This is a refreshing spread for bread, bagels, or any toast. Add a delicate side dish to a salad by spreading the pâté on a slice of French bread, and watch your family smile. In winter this is also delicious alongside a bowl of hearty soup: Spread it on a thick slice of sourdough and broil for two minutes or until bubbly. Mmmm.

8 ounces smoked salmon

8 ounces mascarpone or cream cheese

2 tablespoons minced fresh dill

Zest and juice of ½ lemon

Dash of white pepper

1 tablespoon capers, for garnish

In the bowl of a food processor, place the salmon, mascarpone or cream cheese, dill, lemon juice, and pepper. Pulse until the mixture is well blended.

Scoop into a decorative bowl and cover with plastic wrap. Chill for 30 minutes. Garnish with capers and lemon zest before serving.

HAB-MATO MAYO

MAKES ABOUT 2 CUPS

Use this spicy mayo in place of regular mayonnaise on your favorite sandwich. It gives a little kick that can be amplified with the addition of an extra habanero, if you dare.

1 (or 2) habanero pepper(s), minced

2 cups mayonnaise

1 large tomato, peeled, seeded, and chopped

2 sun-dried tomatoes, finely chopped

Dash of hot pepper sauce or gochujang (Korean red chile paste)

Blend all ingredients together. Chill for 30 minutes for flavors to mellow.

TIP

Note: Wear gloves when working with especially hot peppers to avoid the possibility of unintended and painful burns of sensitive parts.

LEMON-YOGURT BREAD DIP

MAKES ABOUT 2 CUPS

This dip tastes like a creamy lemon Caesar dressing with extra body. The green apple adds both sweet and sour notes, which elevate the flavor to new heights.

Juice and zest of 1 lemon

2 teaspoons hot sauce

3 teaspoons Worcestershire sauce

2 cloves garlic, pressed or finely minced

½ teaspoon freshly cracked black pepper

½ teaspoon sea salt

1 anchovy, finely chopped (optional)

½ cup freshly grated aged provolone or Parmesan cheese

1 small Granny Smith apple, grated on a microplane (must be so fine it almost melts away)

½ cup plain Greek yogurt

½ cup sour cream

1 teaspoon pure maple syrup

1 tablespoon rice vinegar

In a medium mixing bowl, whisk all ingredients together until completely blended. Serve in a bread bowl or decorative dish with chunks of crusty bread for dipping.

OVERSTUFFED PICNIC SANDWICH

MAKES ONE BIG SANDWICH!

Make this sandwich the night before a picnic. It needs to rest, weighted, overnight in the refrigerator. Remember to bring along a cutting board and a sharp knife to your gathering.

1 loaf Borealis bread of your choice

Olive oil to taste

8 cloves roasted garlic, mashed

3 tablespoons basil or other herb pesto

1 pound thinly sliced cold cuts; this combination works well:

    ¼ pound pancetta or prosciutto

    ¼ pound thinly sliced Genoa or hard salami

    ¼ pound ham or sopressata

    ¼ pound capicollo

1 (6-ounce) jar (about 1 cup) artichoke hearts, coarsely chopped

Sun-dried tomatoes packed in oil

Pepperoncini pepper or banana pepper slices

Marinated red peppers

Fresh mozzarella cheese, cut in ½-inch slices

Fresh basil

Crushed red pepper flakes (optional)

Cholula Hot Sauce (optional)

Slice your loaf in half horizontally. Lay cut sides up on a foil-lined cookie sheet. With your fingers, remove some of the soft bread to leave a ½-inch hollow pocket on both the top and bottom pieces. Drizzle both pieces with olive oil, allowing the oil to penetrate the bread.

Spread roasted garlic on the top half of bread and pesto on the bottom half. Layer meats, artichokes, sun-dried tomatoes, peppers, mozzarella, and fresh basil on the bottom half. Drizzle lightly with olive oil after each addition. If you like your sandwiches spicy, add crushed red pepper flakes and a few shakes of Cholula sauce. Place the top of the loaf on the sandwich.

Bring the foil up from under the loaf and wrap it tightly. Place a weight on top of your sandwich—a heavy cast-iron pan works well. Refrigerate overnight. Bring it along to your picnic in a cooler. Slice and serve to your taste buds' delight.

QUICK PICKLED VEGGIES

MAKES ABOUT 2 QUARTS

Every sweet and sour bite adds a note of brightness to your plate. Whether on a sandwich or as part of a platter, pickled veggies are delectable bursts of flavor. I love to up the spicy factor by adding extra peppercorns and Sriracha, sambal oelek, or other chile sauce or paste. Each one adds a different dimension, making the pickles perfect for a cubano, spring roll, panini, or club sandwich.

3 cucumbers, sliced into ⅛-inch coins

1 head cauliflower, cut into 1-inch pieces

3 large tomatoes, seeded and cut into 1-inch pieces

1 pound rainbow carrots, cut into ¼-inch coins

2 cups rice or cider vinegar

4 tablespoons kosher or sea salt

4 tablespoons maple sugar, honey, or maple syrup

1 tablespoon pink, black, or green peppercorns

1 tablespoon dried hibiscus flowers

1 bay leaf

1 tablespoon red pepper flakes

1 tablespoon Sriracha, Cholula, sambal oelek, gochujang, or your favorite chili sauce or paste (optional)

Place vegetables in a large bowl and set aside.

Combine the vinegar, salt, sugar, peppercorns, hibiscus, bay leaf, and red pepper flakes in a saucepan over medium heat. Stir until salt and sugar are dissolved and the mixture has taken on a pink tint from the hibiscus.

Pour vinegar mixture over veggies and let stand for 20 to 30 minutes. Serve immediately or store in a covered jar in the refrigerator for up to a week.

Pizza and Flatbread Toppings

Roasted Heirloom Tomato Sauce

MAKES 3 QUARTS

The gorgeous rainbow of heirloom tomatoes available throughout the summer offers diverse opportunities to vary the flavor and color of this sauce. Simply choosing one hue or another will dramatically accent the sweetness, meatiness, or acidity of your finished product. Inquire at your farmers' market if they have tomatoes for sauce. Often there will be fruit with blemishes that is perfect for this application.

5 pounds ripe heirloom tomatoes, blanched, peeled, cored, seeded, and coarsely chopped

6 medium onions, peeled and coarsely chopped

10 cloves garlic, peeled and coarsely chopped

2 teaspoons salt

1 teaspoon freshly ground black pepper

¼ cup olive oil

3 tablespoons maple sugar

1 cup chopped fresh herbs (parsley, oregano, rosemary, thyme; whatever is on hand or has the flavor you like best)

Preheat the oven to 450°F.

In a large, deep roasting pan, gently toss together the tomatoes, onions, garlic, salt and pepper, and olive oil. Roast, uncovered, for 30 minutes. At the 10-, 20-, and 30-minute marks, thoroughly stir the mixture. Turn the heat down to 400°F. Roast for another 20 minutes, stirring every 5 to 10 minutes. Turn the heat down to 375°F. Add the maple sugar and roast for another 30 minutes, again stirring every 5 to 10 minutes.

Remove from the oven. By this time the tomatoes will have broken down to the sweetest version of themselves. Stir in the herbs; taste and adjust salt and pepper to your liking.

Using a potato masher or immersion blender, macerate the fruit to your preferred texture. For pizza I like to leave larger chunks that lend additional chewiness to the pie. Cool and process in jars or freeze in sturdy ziplock plastic bags.

CHUNKY VEGETABLE MARINARA SAUCE

MAKES 3 QUARTS

Tomato sauce for pizza comes in many shapes and varieties. This recipe is full of chunky veggies, perfect to top your favorite flatbread. If you happen to have the rind from a piece of Parmesan cheese, toss it into the pot with the final ingredients to add a cheesy flavor to the sauce. (Remove the piece of rind that hasn't melted into the sauce before serving.) This sauce freezes well, so make extra to put away for another meal.

½ cup olive oil

1 medium onion, finely chopped

1 cup finely chopped mushrooms

1 cup finely chopped celery

1 cup finely chopped carrots

1 cup finely chopped leeks

30 cloves garlic, peeled and minced

1 tablespoon vegetable bouillon paste (optional)

4 cups diced tomatoes

1 (15-ounce) can tomato paste

1½ cups water

1 tablespoon finely chopped fresh thyme

2 tablespoons finely chopped fresh oregano

¼ cup finely chopped fresh basil

2 bay leaves

½ cup minced fresh parsley

2 tablespoons maple sugar

1 tablespoon sea salt

1 teaspoon black pepper

1 cup dry red wine

Drizzle the oil into a large, heavy saucepan. Over medium-high heat, cook the onions, mushrooms, celery, carrots, leeks, and garlic. Add the bouillon, if using. Cover the pot with a lid and cook, stirring often, for 5 minutes.

Add the diced tomatoes and tomato paste. Bring the sauce to a boil, reduce the heat, and simmer for 1 hour. Add the water, herbs, sugar, salt and pepper, and wine and simmer the sauce for another 60 to 90 minutes, stirring often, until thick and flavorful.

Let the sauce cool. Use immediately, store covered in the refrigerator, freeze, or process in canning jars.

Salsa Fresca

MAKES ABOUT 2 CUPS

Fresh tomatoes lend themselves wonderfully to this bright dish. Use atop grilled seafood or as a dip for tortilla chips, or add six ounces of chopped cooked lobster to the salsa and serve with chips or on crusty bread.

1 cup seeded and diced plum tomatoes

¼ cup minced fresh cilantro leaves

¼ cup finely diced red onion

4 scallions, thinly sliced

1 jalepeño pepper, seeded and finely diced

1 Anaheim pepper, seeded and finely diced

Juice and zest of 1 lime

1 tablespoon cider vinegar

1 teaspoon honey

½ teaspoon sea salt

¼ teaspoon freshly cracked black pepper

Red pepper flakes (optional for more heat)

Mix all ingredients together and chill overnight in a nonmetallic container to blend the flavors.

Béchamel

MAKES 3 QUARTS

Smooth, rich, and creamy, this sauce is an exquisite foundation. Add cheese, pesto, or tomato to create the first layer of a perfect pizza. Melt a bit more cheese and drape it over pasta for the quintessential mac and cheese. Day-old sourdough bread, processed into crumbs, mixed with a bit of melted butter is the perfect topping to baked mac and cheese. Sprinkle the buttered crumbs over the top before baking in a 350°F oven for 15 minutes.

1½ quarts whole milk

1 large onion, halved and peeled

2 bay leaves

1 teaspoon black peppercorns

1 cup (2 sticks) unsalted butter

1 cup flour

1 teaspoon salt, or to taste

½ teaspoon white pepper, or to taste

1 teaspoon nutmeg

In a medium saucepan, heat (scald) the milk with the onion, bay leaves, and peppercorns. Cover, remove from the heat, and let the onion infuse flavor into the milk for 15 minutes.

To make a roux, in a large, heavy-bottomed saucepan, melt the butter over medium-low heat. Once it is hot and bubbly but *not* brown, whisk in the flour and cook, stirring, for about 3 to 4 minutes. Remove from the heat.

Remove the peppercorns, bay leaves, and onion from the milk. Set solids aside for use making stock or in another recipe. Whisk the hot milk into the butter roux.

Return to medium-low heat, whisking constantly, and bring to a gentle boil. Continue whisking until the sauce thickens. Season with salt, pepper, and nutmeg. Stirring constantly, cook until thickened.

BÉCHAMEL VARIATIONS

Pesto Cream Sauce: Whisk ½ cup pesto of your choice into the thickened béchamel sauce. Taste and add more if desired. Season with salt and pepper.

Chive Cream Sauce: Whisk ½ cup minced fresh chives into the thickened béchamel sauce. Taste and add more if desired. Season with salt and pepper.

Cheese Sauce: Whisk in 1 pound finely shredded cheese of your choice. I love the combination of Parmigiano-Reggiano and mozzarella. Pecorino Romano, Asiago, and fontina melt beautifully as well. Smoked Gouda and a pinch of smoked paprika add a depth of flavor that complements the creamy mouth feel. Serve hot.

SOUP'S ON!

HERE ARE A FEW of our favorite soups that utilize the best our local food sources have to offer. There's nothing quite like a grilled cheese on your favorite Borealis bread accompanied by a cup of steaming cream of tomato soup. Here on the coast, seafood is part of the livelihood of our neighbors. We honor it in our Seafood Bisque, incorporating shrimp, scallops, mussels, and oysters. Floating garlic croutons on top of any of these soups adds the proverbial cherry on top.

CREAM OF TOMATO SOUP WITH GARLIC CROUTONS

SERVES 6

This simple, creamy soup is full of flavor. It is delicious warm or at room temperature, by the bowl, or atop a plate of pasta with steamed veggies. Add a touch of garlic oil and a slice of Maine Coast Focaccia (see recipe on page 82) for a complete meal.

1 large Vidalia or sweet onion, minced

3 cloves garlic, minced

3 tablespoons olive oil

1 tablespoon unsalted butter

1 cup vegetable or chicken broth or dry red wine

8 large tomatoes, peeled, seeded, and chopped (approximately 5 cups)

12 large fresh basil leaves

1 teaspoon salt

1 teaspoon white pepper

2 tablespoons maple sugar or honey

2 cups milk, light cream, or plain soymilk

garlic oil for drizzling

Sauté the onions in a large saucepan over medium heat with the garlic, olive oil, and butter. Cook until the onions are transparent, stirring often. Do not let the onions brown.

Deglaze the pan with broth or wine. Stir the onions and liquid well, scraping the bottom to incorporate any brown bits of flavor. Cook on medium-low heat for 10 minutes. Add the tomatoes and cook over low heat another 10 minutes, stirring often.

Wash the basil leaves well and pat dry with paper towels. Stack the leaves one on top of each other on a cutting board. Roll the leaves up into a tight cylinder with the stems at the bottom and the tips at the top. Using a sharp knife and starting at the tips, carefully cut the leaves into ⅛-inch slices. End just before the stems. Set the stems aside (freeze in a ziplock bag for the next time you want extra flavor in your homemade stock). Lift the basil ribbons, called a chiffonade, gently and sprinkle them back down on the cutting board to unfurl and separate them.

Puree the soup; an immersion blender is perfect for blending the soup right in the pan. If you have a regular blender, use caution and puree the hot liquid 1 cup at a time. Return the pureed soup to the pan, add the milk or cream, and stir. Heat the soup on low just until warm enough for your taste.

Ladle the soup into bowls, sprinkle with the fresh basil ribbons, and drizzle with garlic oil. You are ready to eat!

GARLIC OIL— A BREAD'S BEST FRIEND

The recipe for garlic oil is quite simple. For every ½ cup of extra virgin olive oil, mash up, grate, mince, or press two good-size cloves of fresh garlic.

Pour the oil into a bowl, add the garlic, and stir. If you are making this for friends and want them to be impressed and curious about how you got that much flavor into olive oil, heat it gently on the stove with a few peppercorns just until warmed through. This will infuse the oil with a peppery garlic flavor. Let cool and remove the solids by pouring through a fine-mesh strainer. Reserve the solids for use in a dressing or marinade. Use the oil within a day or two. Store any remaining oil in a covered jar in the refrigerator. Bring it to room temperature before serving.

Another way to make garlic oil is to stir the grated or minced garlic and oil together and let sit for 15 minutes or so.

Either way, when you're ready to serve, pour a glistening puddle onto a bread plate or shallow bowl. Grind a few twists of black pepper on the top and sprinkle with coarse sea salt. Dip the edge of a crusty piece of sourdough bread into the oil and delight in its flavor. Delicious! I could eat bread and garlic oil for an entire meal.

GARLIC CROUTONS

SERVES 4–6

This is a great way to use day-old baguettes or any crusty bread. You can even cube your day-old bread and place it in a sealed container in the freezer, to use later when you are ready to make croutons.

1 loaf day-old Borealis rosemary bread, baguette, or whole wheat loaf
4 tablespoons (½ stick) butter
2 cloves garlic, minced
½ teaspoon salt
½ teaspoon white pepper
1 tablespoon chopped fresh (or 1 teaspoon dried) parsley
1 tablespoon chopped fresh (or 1 teaspoon dried) rosemary

Cube the bread to the size you prefer (I like a ½- to ¾-inch cube). Place bread cubes on a cooling rack set on top of a cookie sheet and bake in a 300°F oven for 8 minutes, or until completely dry.

Melt the butter in a microwave-safe dish or in a small saucepan. Add garlic, salt and pepper, and herbs to the butter and stir well.

Pour the crisp bread cubes into a large plastic resealable bag. Pour the butter mixture over the bread in the bag. Seal the bag and shake to coat the bread cubes evenly.

Place the seasoned bread cubes back on the rack on the cookie sheet and bake for an additional 10 minutes. Let cool on the rack and store in the resealable bag you just used or in a sealed container until ready to serve. The flavor is best within a day or two, but if frozen in a sealed bag or container, they will last up to four months.

Roasted Whiskey Maple Sugar-Candied Bacon

The combination of salt, sweet, and fat is either a recipe for bliss or disaster. We're going for rapture! Thick-cut bacon is dusted with maple sugar and the spices of your choice. Feel free to substitute your favorite spicy pepper—cayenne; cracked black, green, or white peppercorns; African Bird Pepper powder; or habanero—and adjust it to tingle or melt your tongue, as desired. The recipe calls for one pound of uncooked bacon. The thicker the cut, the longer the slow roast and the fewer slices for eating. I usually double or triple the recipe. Once that scent of bacony goodness starts wafting around the kitchen, it's hard to keep snitching hands at bay. Crumbling the cooked candied bacon over egg salad on a Borealis slice is the best thing since, well, since sliced bread! Cynthia roasts her candied bacon in the oven and, unlike cooking it in a pan, the bacon lies flat, which makes for easy chopping.

1 pound thick-sliced bacon

1 tablespoon whiskey

3 tablespoons pure Maine maple syrup

½ cup maple sugar

½ cup dark brown sugar

½ teaspoon freshly cracked black pepper or ground pepper of your choice

¼ teaspoon cayenne pepper (optional)

Preheat the oven to 350°F. Line two sheet pans with aluminum foil. The pans should have at least 1-inch sides to contain the rendered fat from the bacon. Set a metal cooling rack on each of the pans. The racks should fit completely inside the pans. If you don't have cooling racks, you can set the coated bacon directly on the foil lining the pan.

Set two pie plates or shallow bowls side by side close to the sheet pans. In one pie plate, add the whiskey and maple syrup and stir until combined. In the second pie plate, stir together the maple sugar, brown sugar, black pepper (or other ground pepper), and cayenne (optional). Shake the dish slightly to make an even surface for the next step.

Separate the slices of bacon and dip each slice in the liquid. Allow any excess liquid to drip back into the pie pan, then press each side of the bacon piece into the sugar and pepper mixture. Carefully lay each slice on the cooling rack in the baking pan, being certain that the strip, as it cooks, will drip any fat into the pan. If your pan is smaller than the bacon slices, cut each slice in half to create two shorter pieces. Don't handle the coated slices too much, as this may cause the sugar to flake off. Try to leave a ½ inch between the raw slices. They will shrink as they cook, but you don't want them to stick together. Repeat with remaining slices of bacon. Discard any leftover maple-whiskey liquid.

Roast the bacon in the preheated oven for 10 minutes. If your oven heats unevenly, you may want to rotate the pans 180 degrees every 5 minutes. At 10 minutes remove one pan at a time and, with tongs, gently turn over each slice. Use caution; any fat on the bacon can drip on the hot foil and spatter. Sprinkle the turned slices with more of the remaining sugar from the coating step above. Return the pans to the oven and roast until the bacon is golden brown and crispy but not burned, another 10 minutes.

Line a large plate with parchment paper or foil. Remove the cooked bacon and let rest and cool on the lined plate for 20 minutes. Save the rendered bacon fat (on the baking pans and plate) in a jar in the refrigerator for future recipes.

Makes the equivalent of 1 pound cooked bacon—the amount depends entirely on how many pieces were snitched to taste! They're irresistible.

PARMESAN ROMANO TOAST

MAKES ABOUT 12–14 TOASTS

Here's another crouton that is fantastic for soups or salads. You can substitute Roquefort, blue cheese, brie, or d'Affinois for the Parmesan and Romano.

1 Borealis baguette

¼ cup olive oil

4 tablespoons (½ stick) softened butter

3 cloves garlic, minced

2 tablespoons finely chopped fresh parsley

2 tablespoons finely chopped fresh basil

½ cup finely grated Parmigiano-Reggiano

½ cup Pecorino Romano

Salt and freshly ground black pepper

Cut the baguette on the diagonal into twelve to fourteen slices.

In a small bowl, combine the oil, butter, garlic, parsley, basil, and Parmesan and Romano cheeses. Mix well. Spread one side of the bread with a generous amount of the mixture. Sprinkle lightly with salt and pepper. Arrange the slices on a baking sheet. Bake at 350°F until golden, about 15 minutes.

SEAFOOD BISQUE

SERVES 4

People travel across the globe for Damariscotta River oysters. The Pemaquid Oyster Festival is held every fall and serves up dishes of all sorts, but this one is a crowd favorite.

1 pound Maine shrimp, cleaned and peeled

1 quart shucked fresh Damariscotta River oysters

2 cups cold water

2 tablespoons finely chopped onions

2 tablespoons cornstarch mixed with 2 tablespoons cold water

2½ cups milk or light cream

2 tablespoons butter

Salt and pepper to taste

1 teaspoon paprika

Dash of Tabasco (optional)

Drain shrimp and oysters in a colander, saving the nectar. Rinse thoroughly. Place shrimp and oysters in a large saucepan. Add the reserved nectar, water, and onions. Boil for 3 to 5 minutes. Remove oysters and shrimp, saving the broth. Bring liquid to a boil, then add cornstarch mixed with water to thicken. Cut oysters into small pieces and return to the pan with the shrimp. Add milk or cream and butter. Season to taste with salt and pepper and paprika, and add a dash of Tabasco if desired. Serve hot with garlic croutons.

BROCCOLI, BEER, AND CHEDDAR SOUP

SERVES 6 GENEROUSLY

The State of Maine Cheese Company has a wonderful assortment of cheddars that are perfect for this soup. I particularly enjoy the Katahdin Cheddar. It melts wonderfully and adds a sumptuous flavor. This soup is especially nice served in a small, hollowed-out bread boule.

3 tablespoons unsalted butter

1 cup finely chopped onion

1 bottle of your favorite beer

2 cups chicken stock

5 large crowns fresh, finely chopped broccoli

8 ounces cream cheese

1 tablespoon chicken bouillon paste or powder

1 cup heavy cream

1 teaspoon salt

10 or so grinds fresh black pepper

Dash of nutmeg

2 cups shredded Katahdin Cheddar plus ¼ cup for garnish

Melt the butter in a large saucepan, then add onions and sauté until translucent. Add beer and stir to deglaze the pan. Add chicken stock and broccoli. Heat to a simmer and cook for 10 minutes. Add cream cheese and bouillon. Stir over low heat until cream cheese is melted. Stir in cream, salt, pepper, and nutmeg. Add shredded cheese and heat on low, stirring constantly until cheese is melted and incorporated.

Using an immersion blender, puree the soup in the pan to the consistency you desire. You may also puree the soup in small batches in a blender, then return the soup to the pan. If you prefer the soup chunky, feel free to skip this step.

Keep soup warm on very low heat until you are ready to serve. Garnish with remaining shredded Katahdin Cheddar.

WILD FIVE MUSHROOM SOUP

SERVES 8

Welcome to the wild side. This soup is a forager's delight. Be sure to purchase your mushrooms from a reputable source. The amount of each variety is up to you. The total five cups of chopped mushrooms can be all one type or a bit of a dozen different kinds. Adding the nutty wild rice gives this soup an extra dimension, faceted by the textures and shapes of the assorted mushrooms. Serve with a slice of Borealis potato bread and sweet butter.

6 tablespoons unsalted butter

½ cup minced shallot

½ teaspoon sea salt

1 cup roughly chopped cremini mushrooms

1 cup roughly chopped oyster mushrooms

1 cup roughly chopped maitake or matsutake mushrooms

1 cup roughly chopped portobello mushrooms

1 cup roughly chopped shiitake mushrooms

1 cup wild rice

1 tablespoon chicken or vegetable bouillon paste or powder

8 cups chicken stock

1 pound Maine potatoes, cut into bite-size chunks

1 tablespoon minced fresh sage

1 tablespoon minced fresh rosemary

3 tablespoons minced garlic

1 teaspoon sea salt

1 teaspoon freshly cracked black pepper

½ teaspoon white pepper

½ cup snipped fresh chives, divided

2 cups light cream

½ cup finely chopped fresh parsley

2 ounces enoki mushrooms, for garnish

Melt the butter in a large, heavy-bottomed saucepan over medium-high heat. Add shallots and ½ teaspoon sea salt. Sauté for 3 minutes. Add all mushrooms, wild rice, and the bouillon. Sauté for 5 minutes. Stir in chicken stock and potatoes. Bring to a boil, then reduce heat, cover, and simmer for 30 minutes. Add sage, rosemary, and garlic.

With a potato masher, gently press the solids and "mash" the potatoes in the soup. Stir well after mashing, being sure to scrape up and incorporate all the bits from the bottom of the pan. Return to low heat and cook for 15 minutes longer, stirring often. Add the salt, black and white pepper, and 3 tablespoons of the snipped chives. Stir in the cream.

Once heated through it's ready to serve. Garnish each dish with a sprinkle of parsley, snipped chives, and a few enoki mushrooms. If you're feeling fancy, save a few long pieces of chive and tie up a little bundle of enoki mushrooms to top each bowl.

TWO POTATO SOUP

SERVES 6

Potato soup is the ultimate comfort food. Creamy and hearty, it's perfect for a snowy winter day. This version uses two different varieties of potato.

8 medium russet potatoes, peeled and chopped
4 medium fingerling potatoes, peeled and chopped
3 scallions, finely sliced
1 tablespoon minced garlic
1 tablespoon salt
1½ tablespoons freshly cracked black pepper
4 cups light cream
1½ cups freshly grated Asiago cheese

Boil potatoes in a large, heavy-bottomed saucepan. Drain, reserving 1 cup of the cooking water. Return the reserved water to the pan and mash the potatoes until smooth. Add the scallions, garlic, salt, pepper, and cream. Cook on low heat for 20 minutes.

Add Asiago cheese just before serving. Turn off the heat and allow cheese to melt into the soup. Stir well to incorporate.

Once the cheese is melted, the soup is ready to serve. Garnish with cracked black pepper.

ON THE SIDE

BREAD AND TOMATO SALAD

SERVES 6–8

Panzanella is a traditional Italian bread and tomato salad dressed with a simple vinaigrette. Here in Maine we have Fiore, an extraordinary importer of olive oils and vinegars. At Fiore you can find dozens of naturally infused flavors in both lines, from blood orange oil and grapefruit white balsamic to Herbs de Provence oil and dark chocolate aged balsamic. Simply incredible.

Salad
3 pounds ripe red, orange, and yellow tomatoes, cut in 1-inch chunks

1 cup basil leaves, torn into small pieces

1 cup flat-leaf parsley

¼ cup minced sweet onion

1 teaspoon coarse sea salt

Croutons
3 cups Borealis French Peasant or Aroostook Wheat bread, crusts removed and cut into 2-inch cubes

3 tablespoons fruity extra virgin olive oil

3 cloves garlic, minced or grated

Dressing
2 cloves garlic, thinly sliced

3 tablespoons balsamic vinegar

½ cup fruity olive oil (Fiore has a Tuscan Herb oil perfect for this dish.)

1 teaspoon sea salt

1 teaspoon freshly cracked black pepper

In a large bowl, combine the tomatoes, basil, parsley, onion, and salt. Let stand at room temperature until ready to serve.

Preheat the oven to 400°F. In another bowl, toss the bread cubes, olive oil, and minced garlic together until bread is evenly coated. Place mixture on a sheet pan lined with parchment and toast for 15 minutes, stirring once during baking, until golden.

For the dressing, combine the sliced garlic, vinegar, olive oil, salt, and pepper. Pour over the salad ingredients immediately before serving and toss to coat. Add the croutons and toss once more.

GORGONZOLA CREAM DRESSING

MAKES ABOUT 3 CUPS

This is a silky, savory dressing that is perfect for a salad or to spread on half a loaf of bread and broil until bubbly. The recipe is for a small batch; feel free to multiply if you need more.

1 cup real mayonnaise

1 cup sour cream

¼ cup light cream

1 tablespoon sugar

½ teaspoon salt

1 teaspoon freshly cracked black or white pepper

1 teaspoon garlic powder, or 1 small clove garlic, minced

2 tablespoons champagne vinegar

8 ounces crumbled Gorgonzola cheese

Whisk together the mayo, sour cream, light cream, sugar, salt and pepper, and garlic. Add the vinegar and whisk again. Fold in the cheese. Serve with your choice of vegetables or bread.

MAPLE KETCHUP

MAKES ABOUT 2 CUPS

Here is an answer to your condiment conundrum: Create your own ketchup using rich, pure Maine maple syrup. No high-fructose corn syrup here, just local, natural gold!

2 tablespoons olive oil
1 medium onion, finely chopped
1 (28-ounce) can whole tomatoes
3 tablespoons tomato paste
½ cup pure maple syrup
1 tablespoon molasses
½ cup cider vinegar
½ teaspoon salt

Heat oil in a large, heavy-bottomed pan. Sauté onions until soft, about 8 minutes. Meanwhile, puree tomatoes in a blender. When onions are soft, add pureed tomatoes, tomato paste, syrup, molasses, vinegar, and salt. Simmer for approximately 1 hour, stirring occasionally. Remove from the heat.

Once mixture has cooled slightly, puree in batches. Cool for 2 hours before serving. Ketchup will keep for up to 3 weeks if refrigerated in a well-sealed container.

Variations

- Toast one or two dried ancho chile peppers. Remove seeds, roughly chop, and add to mixture before simmering. Peppers will soften and puree with other ingredients.

- Add 2 teaspoons hot smoked paprika before simmering.

- Grate a 1-inch piece of ginger and sauté with onions.

- Add 1–2 teaspoons Sriracha before simmering.

- Add 2 tablespoons gochujang (Korean red chile paste).

SPINACH AND BASIL PESTO

MAKES ABOUT 2 CUPS

For those who love spinach, this pesto packs a punch. Brilliant emerald, it retains its color from the addition of fresh lemon juice. The secret is to reserve a tablespoon or two. Once you're finished making your batch, place the pesto in a jar and float the reserved lemon juice on top. This will prevent the leaves from oxidizing and discoloring. Store covered in the refrigerator. To freeze, carefully spread pesto into a clean ice cube tray. Once frozen, pop the cubes out of the tray and into a ziplock bag or other storage container. The pesto will keep for months until needed for your favorite dish.

2 cups (packed) fresh basil

3 cups (packed) fresh baby spinach (in a pinch you can substitute frozen spinach)

½ cup fresh flat-leaf parsley (leaves only)

12 peeled cloves garlic

1 teaspoon salt

¼ cup fresh lemon juice (plus another tablespoon or so for the top)

⅓ cup extra virgin olive oil

1 cup grated Parmesan cheese

Place the washed basil, spinach, and parsley in a food processor and begin to puree. Add the garlic and salt. Continue to puree. With the machine running, drizzle in the lemon juice and oil. Scrape down the sides to be sure all ingredients are incorporated. Add the cheese and pulse until completely blended. If the pesto is dry, add a bit more oil. It should be a moist paste when you're finished.

Place pesto in a glass container and drizzle the top with a bit more lemon juice to prevent discoloration. Cover and chill until ready to use.

BASIL GARLIC SCAPE PESTO

MAKES ABOUT 2 CUPS

Make this pesto using garlic scapes and basil for a spectacular burst of flavor. If you are watching calories, you can substitute chicken broth for the olive oil. Toss with pasta—warm or cold—for a fantastic dish. Stir into olive oil to marinate mozzarella, or add just a little extra oil and use the mixture for dipping crusty bread at the table.

2 cups fresh basil leaves

12 garlic scapes, chopped

2 cloves garlic

½ cup grated Parmesan cheese

½ cup flax seeds, chia seeds, pine nuts, or walnuts

½ cup extra virgin olive oil

Salt and black pepper to taste

Combine basil, scapes, garlic, cheese, and seeds or nuts in a food processor. Pulse to blend. With the motor running, slowly add the olive oil. Season to taste with salt and pepper and process to the desired consistency.

ROSEMARY PESTO

MAKES ABOUT 1 CUP

Great on lamb and buffalo, this pesto is robust and flavorful. Mix it into cream cheese, or spread on halves of crusty sourdough bread and broil until bubbly to serve alongside burgers in the summer.

½ cup (packed) parsley leaves and stems

3 tablespoons chopped fresh rosemary plus rosemary sprigs

2 cloves garlic

4 tablespoons grated Parmesan cheese

3 tablespoons extra virgin olive oil

Salt and black pepper to taste

Combine parsley, rosemary, garlic, and cheese in a food processor. Pulse to mix. With the machine running, slowly add the olive oil. Season to taste with salt and pepper and process to the desired consistency.

SAGE PESTO

MAKES ABOUT 1 CUP

Excellent tucked under the skin of chicken breasts or mixed with pine nuts and fresh bread crumbs as a stuffing for pork chops.

½ cup fresh sage leaves

1½ cups fresh parsley

2 cloves garlic

½ cup pine nuts or walnuts

½ cup grated Parmesan cheese

½ cup extra virgin olive oil

Salt and black pepper to taste

Combine sage, parsley, garlic, nuts, and cheese in a food processor. Pulse to mix. With the machine running, slowly add the olive oil. Season to taste with salt and pepper and process to the desired consistency.

ORANGE MINT PESTO

MAKES ABOUT 1 CUP

This bright, fresh pesto is lovely on pasta, mixed with sour cream as a dip for cooked tortellini, swirled into mascarpone cheese for a cracker spread, or even mixed with ½ cup powdered sugar and whipped cream to top a fruit tart.

1¼ cups fresh mint leaves

1 cup fresh parsley

½ cup chia seeds, pine nuts, or walnuts

Juice and zest of 1 orange

1 tablespoon frozen orange juice concentrate

¼ cup extra virgin olive oil

Pinch of sea salt and white pepper

Combine mint, parsley, chia or nuts, orange zest, and orange juice concentrate in a food processor. Pulse to mix. With the motor running, slowly add the fresh orange juice and olive oil. Season to taste with salt and white pepper and process to the desired consistency.

PEPITA PESTO

MAKES ABOUT 1 CUP

Pumpkin seeds are nutty and bright, reminiscent of fall baking. Using pepitas in place of nuts makes for a lovely, hearty pesto that will stand up to other ingredients.

½ cup extra virgin olive oil, divided
2 cups hulled pumpkin seeds
2 shallots, finely chopped
4 cloves garlic, finely chopped
½ teaspoon sea salt
Freshly cracked black pepper
½ cup chopped flat-leaf parsley
1 tablespoon chopped fresh sage
5 ounces soft goat cheese
½ cup water
5 tablespoons fresh lemon juice

In a large skillet, heat 2 tablespoons of the olive oil over medium heat. Add the pumpkin seeds and cook, stirring, until they begin to turn golden brown, about 5 minutes. Use caution, as some may spit or pop from the pan. Add the shallots and garlic and cook until softened, about 2 minutes. Season with sea salt and pepper and transfer to a plate to cool for 10 minutes.

Place the pumpkin seed mixture into the bowl of a food processor along with the parsley, sage, goat cheese, water, and lemon juice. Pulse until pesto is a uniform consistency, scraping down the sides of the bowl as needed. With the machine running, drizzle in the remaining olive oil and process until the mixture becomes a thick paste. Transfer to a bowl; taste and adjust seasonings if necessary.

CILANTRO CITRUS PESTO

MAKES ABOUT 2 CUPS

Refreshing and delicious, this pesto will brighten up a plate of pasta or vegetables. Mix with mascarpone and spread on a tortilla to add flavor to a quesadilla, or spread on toast or a sandwich.

2 cups fresh cilantro

½ cup fresh baby spinach

½ cup fresh parsley

3 cloves garlic

Zest and juice of 1 lemon

Zest and juice of 1 lime

½ cup toasted pine nuts or sunflower seeds

½ cup olive oil

½ cup grated or shredded Parmesan cheese

Pinch of sea salt and white pepper

Combine cilantro, spinach, parsley, garlic, citrus juice and zest, and nuts or seeds in a food processor. Pulse to mix. With the motor running, slowly add the olive oil, then the Parmesan cheese. Season to taste with salt and white pepper and process to the desired consistency.

PESTO RICOTTA

MAKES ABOUT 1½ CUPS

This mixture is a wonderful layer in lasagne, in stuffed shells, or atop pizza. It's especially delicious stirred into mashed potatoes or spread on a thick slice of baguette.

1 cup ricotta cheese

1 handful (about ¼ cup) fresh basil leaves, chopped fine

¼ cup grated Parmesan or Asiago cheese

Salt and pepper to taste

Combine all ingredients in a small bowl and stir until basil is completely incorporated. Chill until ready to use.

CHEESE IN HERBED OIL

MAKES ABOUT 2 CUPS HERB OIL PLUS CHEESE

This herb oil will strengthen as it sits, and the cheese will become more infused with the flavors. It's delicious in salads or as an appetizer.

2 cups olive oil
2 cloves garlic
1 sprig fresh thyme
1 sprig fresh rosemary
1 bay leaf
1 teaspoon red pepper flakes, or 1 dried chile pepper
6 black peppercorns
6 red peppercorns
1 pound feta or other fresh soft cheese, chopped into bite-size pieces

Place all ingredients in a wide-mouth jar with a lid. This recipe wil keep refrigerated for 1 to 2 months. Bring to room temperature before serving.

Sweet and Savory Herb Butters

HERB BUTTER

MAKES ABOUT 1 CUP

Herbed butters can easily replace regular butter in recipes for soups, gravies, sauces, or on bread, vegetables, rice, or pasta. They can be frozen or will store in the refrigerator for two to three weeks. Unsalted butter is preferred because it allows for the fullest herb flavor, and salt and pepper can be added to taste. Fresh herbs should be washed and dried before chopping and snipping, while dry herbs should be pulverized. Parsley enhances the flavor of all herbs. Other possibilities are Parmesan cheese, nuts, dry mustard, curry powder, celery seed, hot pepper sauce, smoked paprika, orange or lemon zest, and scallions.

Two of our favorite combinations are marjoram, roasted garlic, parsley, and lemon zest; and tarragon, fennel, parsley, and lemon zest.

1 cup (2 sticks) unsalted butter, softened

3 tablespoons chopped fresh herbs, or 3 teaspoons dried herbs

1 tablespoon fresh lemon juice

Salt and pepper to taste

With a spoon, blend herbs, lemon juice, and salt and pepper into softened butter. Refrigerate overnight for flavors to mix. Taste the next day and add more herbs if needed for additional flavor. If flavors are too strong, stir in another 2 tablespoons butter. Serve at room temperature.

LEMON PESTO BUTTER

MAKES ABOUT 1 CUP

Simple and flavorful, use this herb butter in place of regular butter at the table or in your favorite savory recipe.

1 cup (2 sticks) unsalted butter, softened

3 tablespoons pesto or chopped fresh herbs

1 tablespoon fresh lemon juice

1 tablespoon hot pepper sauce

Sea salt and pepper to taste

With a spoon, blend the pesto or herbs, lemon juice, hot sauce, and salt and pepper into softened butter. Place in a covered container. Refrigerate overnight to allow flavors to mingle. Taste the next day and add more pesto or herbs if needed for additional flavor. Serve at room temperature.

ORANGE BUTTER

MAKES ABOUT 1 CUP

1 cup (2 sticks) unsalted butter, softened

1 tablespoon orange zest

¼ cup fresh orange juice

1 tablespoon frozen orange juice concentrate

In a small bowl, mix together the softened butter, orange zest, orange juice, and orange juice concentrate. Serve at room temperature.

SWEET LEMON BUTTER

MAKES ABOUT 1 CUP

1 cup (2 sticks) unsalted butter, softened

3 tablespoons lemon zest

¼ cup fresh lemon juice

3 tablespoons maple sugar or honey

½ teaspoon sea salt

In a small bowl, mix together the softened butter, lemon zest, lemon juice, sugar or honey, and salt. If serving immediately, spoon into a small bowl. Set aside at room temperature.

If serving later, this recipe refrigerates and freezes well. Lay out an 8 × 11-inch piece of parchment on a flat surface. Shape mixture into a log and place in the center of one of the long sides of the parchment. Bring the paper up and around the roll, tucking the edge under the butter. Slowly roll up the paper, encasing the butter. (Remember, the heat from your hands will melt the butter.)

FAIRY BUTTER CURLS

MAKES ABOUT ¾ CUP

This delicate sweet butter can be shaved or grated (if you first place it in the freezer for an hour) to add a special bit of richness. It's lovely on French toast made with your favorite Borealis sourdough bread.

½ cup (1 stick) unsalted butter, softened
4 tablespoons maple sugar
1 tablespoon pure vanilla extract
¼ teaspoon salt

Cream the butter, sugar, vanilla, and salt. Scrape the mixture into the bottom of a ziplock bag. Press the mixture compactly into a long roll. With the bag open, roll it up, expelling any air from around the butter. Zip the bag closed and chill or freeze until ready to use.

To make butter curls, first chill a small bowl. Remove the butter from the refrigerator or freezer. Working quickly, unwrap the roll. Using a vegetable peeler, gently scrape a thin strip of butter off the side of the roll. The thin pieces should curl. Set aside in the chilled bowl. Cover and chill until ready to use.

ON THE SWEET SIDE

SPICED RUM HONEY

MAKES ABOUT 1 PINT

Here's something special to put in your tea or spread on toast.

2 cups honey

2 cinnamon sticks

3 tablespoons dark rum

4 whole cardamom pods, crushed in your palm

1 teaspoon ground cinnamon

4 sprigs or 8-10 leaves lemon basil

Pour the honey into a small saucepan. Add the cinnamon sticks, dark rum, cardamom pods, and cinnamon or lemon basil. Heat gently until it becomes fluid. Place basil leaves in a clean 16-ounce jar and pour the warmed honey mixture over them. Cover and store in a clean dry place to steep for at least a week before using.

MINTED HONEY

MAKES 1 PINT

Enjoy this honey stirred into tea, spread on toast, or drizzled on fresh fruit.

2 cups honey

2 leaves fresh spearmint or peppermint, cleaned and dried

Pour honey into a small saucepan and heat gently. Place mint leaves in a clean 16-ounce jar and pour the warmed honey over them. Cover and store in a clean dry place to steep for at least a week before using.

GINGER WASABI MAPLE SYRUP

MAKES 1 PINT

This spicy-sweet syrup is a great addition to marinades and salad dressings. Delicious drizzled on French toast and even on scrambled eggs, it brings the sweet and savory together in one luscious bite. The Grade A dark robust Maine maple syrup gives the richest depth of flavor.

2 cups pure Maine maple syrup

1 teaspoon wasabi paste

6 (¼-inch-thick) slices fresh ginger root

Heat maple syrup in a small saucepan with the wasabi and ginger. When heated through, remove from the heat and let cool. Store in a covered glass jar in the refrigerator.

MAPLE SEA SALT CARAMEL SAUCE

MAKES ABOUT 2 CUPS

Caramel sauce is good on most anything. From popcorn to cheesecake, French toast to bread pudding, ice cream to potato chips, the balance of sweet, salty, and rich is hard to resist. Fold it into whipped cream and toasted coconut for a delicious frosting for cupcakes. Spoon over brownies topped with slices of banana. Dip pretzel sticks and drizzle with melted peanut butter for an easy dessert treat.

2 cups whipping cream

¾ cup sugar

½ cup maple sugar

½ cup pure maple syrup

1 vanilla bean, halved

4 tablespoons (½ stick) unsalted butter

1 teaspoon coarse sea salt

Combine cream, sugars, and syrup in a heavy-bottomed medium saucepan. Stir over medium heat until sugar dissolves. Add vanilla bean. Increase heat and bring to a boil. Reduce heat to medium-low and simmer the sauce until caramel has colored and thickened, whisking often, about 35 minutes. Stir in butter until melted and incorporated. Cool slightly. Gently stir in sea salt. Remove vanilla bean (save in a ziplock bag in the freezer to flavor another recipe).

Caramel sauce can be made up to 3 days ahead, just cover and chill. When ready to use, warm over medium heat, stirring; add 2 tablespoons hot water if necessary to dissolve any crystallized sugar.

TOMATO MEMBRILLO

MAKES ABOUT 2 CUPS

Quince paste, membrillo *in Spanish, is a thick fruit and sugar puree that's delicious with cheese and bread. This recipe uses tomato instead of quince. The pectin in the tomato skin helps to thicken the mixture. It's one of those three-ingredient magic tricks where a little bit of time yields a spectacular result.*

4 cups tomato skins, seeds, and pulp

2 cups sugar

¼ teaspoon sea salt

Place tomato, sugar, and salt in a medium saucepan. Heat until mixture comes to a boil, stirring often. Reduce heat and cook, stirring frequently, until reduced by half. Cool for 30 minutes.

Blend or puree, then strain thickened mixture through a fine-mesh sieve. Pour into an oiled loaf pan. Chill. Serve spread on crackers with cheese or in place of jam in your favorite dish.

CASHEW PUMPKIN GOAT CHEESE SPREAD

MAKES ABOUT 3 CUPS

This high-protein spread can tip toward sweet or savory by adjusting just one ingredient. The maple syrup can be reduced or increased by half, with dramatic results. If you prefer a vegan dish, omit the chèvre and substitute silken tofu.

1½ cups raw cashews

¼ cup water

1 cup pumpkin puree

1 teaspoon ground cinnamon

1 tablespoon grated fresh ginger

½ teaspoon grated fresh nutmeg

½ teaspoon salt

¼ cup maple syrup (Grade A dark robust gives the richest flavor)

8 ounces goat cheese

Puree the cashews and water in a food processor or blender until smooth. Add pumpkin, spices, salt, maple syrup, and goat cheese and puree, scraping sides down frequently, until mixture is smooth and uniform. Serve chilled with bread rounds.

Borealis Breads Maple Granola

MAKES ABOUT 5 POUNDS

This is not your everyday, run-of-the-mill toasted oats and just a whisper of other ingredients granola! Not when the third ingredient by weight is maple syrup. Yes, this granola is on the sweet side, but oh so good! It's tasty straight or with yogurt and fresh Maine blueberries. We even stir it into our favorite muffin batter before baking from time to time, adding an extra crunch to the soft, cakey goodness.

6 cups rolled oats
4 cups chopped walnuts
2¾ cups dried cranberries
⅓ cup brown sugar
4 cups pure Maine maple syrup
1 cup canola oil

Preheat the oven to 325°F. Line a sheet pan with parchment paper.

Measure oats, walnuts, cranberries, and brown sugar into a large bowl, breaking up any chunks of brown sugar by hand. Add syrup and oil and mix for 2 minutes or less, just until moistened. Scrape sides down and mix for another 10 seconds.

Scoop mixture onto the prepared sheet pan. Plan to stay near the oven to watch the granola. It demands attention, especially toward the end of its baking.

Bake for about 35 minutes, rotating the pan often. It takes about five rotations to fully cook. First, bake for 10 minutes. Rotate the pan 180 degrees, then bake again for another 10 minutes. The third, fourth, and fifth rotations bake 5 minutes each. This is a guideline; each batch is judged on its own. As you bake the granola, at each rotation take the pan out of the oven briefly and stir by carefully folding the corners and edges of parchment paper into the center. Gently shake the pan to maneuver the mixture back into an even layer of ingredients. The granola should be toasted and aromatic, but not burned (a convection oven is helpful to keep the air moving).

When finished baking, let cool completely before storing in an airtight container.

PUMPKIN MAPLE BREAD PUDDING

SERVES 6

This dessert is a winning combination of custard and French toast. Made with Borealis Breads' Pumpkin Raisin loaves (see recipe on page 67), we've added spices to complement the bread perfectly.

1 cup pure maple syrup, divided, or 1 cup maple sugar

1 tablespoon fresh lemon juice

6 slices Borealis Breads' Pumpkin Raisin bread, with or without crusts

2 tablespoons butter, room temperature

1 cup pumpkin puree

4 eggs plus 2 egg yolks

2 cups light cream

1 teaspoon ground cinnamon

½ teaspoon nutmeg

¼ teaspoon sea salt

2 teaspoons pure vanilla extract or rum

½ cup currants, golden raisins, or dried cranberries

Preheat the oven to 325°F. Grease a 3-quart baking dish. Pour ¾ cup maple syrup and the lemon juice in the bottom of the dish. Butter each slice of bread and cut into ¾-inch cubes. Set aside.

In a medium bowl, whisk together the pumpkin puree, eggs, egg yolks, cream, cinnamon, nutmeg, sea salt, and vanilla or rum. Add bread cubes and toss just until coated. Pour mixture into the baking dish.

At this point you can cover and chill overnight or proceed. Bake for 1 hour. Drizzle baked bread pudding with another ¼ cup maple syrup and serve.

WINTER SPICE BLEND

MAKES ABOUT 1 CUP

When the world goes to the pumpkins, here's an alternative that gives a warm spice to your favorite dish. Enjoy this spicy sweetness in your latte or hot chocolate, mix with vanilla yogurt, stir into granola, or my favorite, sprinkle on buttered toast.

¼ cup ground cinnamon

2 tablespoons ground ginger

1 tablespoon ground nutmeg

1 tablespoon ground cardamom

½ cup maple sugar

Mix all ingredients together. Store in an airtight container. Shake before using.

SWEET CINNAMON HAZELNUTS

MAKES ABOUT 4 CUPS

If you love spiced nuts, welcome home. These can be made ahead and kept in a sealed container for two weeks. They usually don't last that long! Feel free to substitute pecans, walnuts, or mixed nuts.

1 cup sugar

½ cup cold water

¾ teaspoon coarse sea salt

1 teaspoon pure vanilla extract

1 teaspoon ground cinnamon or cardamom

4 cups hazelnuts

In a medium saucepan, combine the sugar, water, and salt. Bring to a boil and cook without stirring until the mixture reaches 240°F on a candy thermometer, about 4 minutes. Add the vanilla and cinnamon or cardamom and stir until blended. The mixture may bubble up and splatter, so be careful. Add the nuts. Stir to coat evenly, then immediately pour out onto a cookie sheet lined with parchment or waxed paper. Cool until easy to handle.

If necessary, break nuts apart before serving. Serve on top of or as an accompaniment to your favorite salad.

MAINE GRAIN AND EDUCATIONAL RESOURCES

Borealis Breads
1860 Atlantic Highway
Waldoboro, ME 04572
(207) 832-0655
1165 Post Rd.
Wells, ME
(207) 641-8800

Aurora Mills and Farm
Matthew Williams and
Sara Williams Flewelling
408 Burton Rd.
Linneus, ME 04730
www.AuroraMillsandFarm.com

MOFGA
PO Box 170
Unity, ME 04988
(207) 568-4142
294 Crosby Brook Rd.
Unity, ME
www.mofga.org

The Kneading Conference
Kennebec Valley Community College
677 Skowhegan Rd.
Clinton, ME
www.KneadingConference.com

Maine Grains Alliance
PO Box 2060
Skowhegan, ME 04976
(207) 474-8001
amber@mainegrains.com

Somerset Grist Mill
42 Court St.
Skowhegan, ME 04976
(207) 474-8001

Songbird Farm
142 Stevens Rd.
Unity, ME 04988
(207) 380-1171
songbird.farm@yahoo.com

University of Maine Cooperative Extension Service
5741 Libby Hall
Orono, ME 04469-5741
(207) 581-3188 or (800) 287-0274
(in Maine)
https://extension.umaine.edu

Maine Department of Agriculture, Conservation and Forestry
32 Blossom Ln.
Marquardt Building
Augusta, ME Kennebec
(207) 287-3491
www.getrealmaine.com